C000064913

بسم الله الرحمن الرحيم

ABOUT THE AUTHOR

Under the pen-name HARUN YAHYA, the author has published many books on political and faith-related issues. An important body of his work deals with the materialistic world view and the impact of it in world history and politics. (The pen-name is formed from the names 'Harun' [Aaron] and 'Yahya' [John] in the esteemed memory of the two Prophets who struggled against infidelity.)

His works include The 'Secret Hand' in Bosnia, The Holocaust Hoax, Behind the Scenes of Terrorism, Israel's Kurdish Card, A National Strategy for Turkey, Solution: The Morals of the Qur'an, Darwin's Antagonism Against the Turks, The Evolution Deceit, Perished Nations, The Golden Age, The Art of Colour by Allah, The Truth of the Life of This World, Confessions of Evolutionists, The Blunders of Evolutionists, The Qur'an Leads the Way to Science, The Real Origin of Life, Miracles of the Qur'an, The Design in Nature, Self-Sacrifice and Intelligent Behaviour Models in Animals, Eternity Has Already Begun, Children Darwin Was Lying!, The End of Darwinism, The Creation of the Universe, Never Plead Ignorance, Timelessness and the Reality of Fate, The Miracle of the Atom, The Miracle in the Cell, The Miracle of the Immune System, The Miracle in the Eye, The Creation Miracle in Plants, The Miracle in the Spider, The Miracle in the Ant, The Miracle in the Gnat, The Miracle in the Honeybee.

Among his booklets are The Mystery of the Atom, The Collapse of the Theory of Evolution: The Fact of Creation, The Collapse of Materialism, The End of Materialism, The Blunders of Evolutionists 1, The Blunders of Evolutionists 2, The Microbiological Collapse of Evolution, The Fact of Creation, The Collapse of the Theory of Evolution in 20 Questions, The Biggest Deception in the History of Biology: Darwinism.

The author's other works on Quranic topics include: Ever Thought About the Truth?, Devoted to Allah, Abandoning the Society of Ignorance, Paradise, The Theory of Evolution, The Moral Values of the Qur'an, Knowledge of the Qur'an, Qur'an Index, Emigrating for the Cause of Allah, The Character of Hypocrites in the Qur'an, The Secrets of the Hypocrite, The Names of Allah, Communicating the Message and Disputing in the Qur'an, The Basic Concepts in the Qur'an, Answers from the Qur'an, Death Resurrection Hell, The Struggle of the Messengers, The Avowed Enemy of Man: Satan, Idolatry, The Religion of the Ignorant, The Arrogance of Satan, Prayer in the Qur'an, The Importance of Conscience in the Qur'an, The Day of Resurrection, Never Forget, Disregarded Judgements of the Qur'an, Human Characters in the Society of Ignorance, The Importance of Patience in the Qur'an, General Information from the Qur'an, Quick Grasp of Faith 1-2-3, The Crude Reasoning of Disbelief, The Mature Faith, Before You Regret, Our Messengers Say, The Mercy of Believers, The Fear of Allah, The Nightmare of Disbelief, Prophet Isa Will Come, Beauties Presented by the Qur'an for Life, The Iniquity Called "Mockery", The Secret of the Test, The True Wisdom According to the Qur'an, The Struggle with the Religion of Irreligion, Bouquet of the Beauties of Allah 1-2-3-4.

DEEP THINKING

Copyright © Harun Yahya 2000 CE
First Published by Vural Yayıncılık, İstanbul, Turkey in September 1999

First English Edition published in April 2000

Published by:
Ta-Ha Publishers Ltd.
1 Wynne Road
London SW9 OBB

Website: http://www.taha.co.uk
E-Mail: sales @ taha.co.uk

All rights reserved. No part of this publication may be reproduced, stored in any retrivial system or
transmitted in any form or by any methods, electronic, mechanical, photocopying, recording, or
otherwise without the prior permission of the publishers.

By Harun Yahya
Translated By: Mustapha Ahmad
Edited By: Abdassamad Clarke

A catalog record of this book is available from the British Library
ISBN 1 84200 00 9 8

Printed and bound by:
Secil Ofset in İstanbul
Address: Yüzyıl Mahallesi MAS-SIT Matbaacılar Sitesi
4. Cadde No:77 Bağcılar- İstanbul / TURKEY

Website: http: // www.harunyahya.org - http: // www.harunyahya.com
http: // www.harunyahya.net

DEEP
THINKING

*Those who remember Allah, standing,
sitting, and lying on their sides, and reflect
on the creation of the heavens and the
earth: "O Lord, You have not created this
for nothing. Glory be to You! So safeguard
us from the punishment of the Fire."
(Surat Al 'Imran: 191)*

HARUN YAHYA

Ta-Ha Publishers Ltd.
I Wynne Road London SW9 OBB
United Kingdom

TO THE READER

In all the books by the author, faith-related issues are told in the light of the Qur'anic verses and people are invited to learn Allah's words and to live by them. All the subjects that concern Allah's verses are explained in such a way as to leave no room for doubt or question marks in the reader's mind. The sincere, plain and fluent style employed ensures that everyone of every age and from every social group can easily understand the books. This effective and lucid way of recounting makes the books read suitable for reading in a single sitting. Even those who rigorously reject spirituality are influenced by the facts recounted in these books and cannot refute the truthfulness of their contents.

This book and all the other works of the author can be read by individuals or studied in a group at a time of conversation. The reading of the books by a group of readers willing to profit from them will be useful in the sense that readers can relate their own reflections and experiences to one another.

In addition, it will be a great service to the religion to contribute to the presentation and reading of these books, which are written solely for the good pleasure of Allah. All the books of the author are extremely convincing. For this reason, for those who want to communicate the religion to other people, one of the most effective methods is to encourage them to read these books.

Contents

Introduction 8

Deep Thinking 12

What Do People Usually Think About? 22

What are the Reasons that Prevent Thought? 26

Those Things that Need to be Thought About 36

Thinking Over the Verses of the Qur'an 88

Conclusion 100

Introduction

*H*ave you ever thought about the fact that you did not exist before you were conceived and then born into the world and that you have come into existence from mere nothingness?

Have you ever thought about how the flowers you see in your living room everyday come out of pitch black, muddy soil with fragrant smells and are as colourful as they are?

Have you ever thought about how mosquitoes, which irritatingly fly around you, move their wings so fast that we are unable to see them?

Have you ever thought about how the peels of fruits such as bananas, watermelons, melons and oranges serve as wrappings of high quality, and how the fruits are packed in these wrappings so that they maintain their taste and fragrance?

Have you ever thought about the possibility that while you are asleep a sudden earthquake could raze your home, your office, and your city to the ground and that in a few seconds you could lose everything of the world you possess?

Have you ever thought of how your life passes away very quickly, and that you will grow old and become weak, and slowly lose your beauty, health and strength?

Have you ever thought about how one day you will find the angels of death appointed by Allah before you and that you will then leave this world?

Well, have you ever thought about why people are so attached to a world from which they will soon depart when what they basically need is to strive for the hereafter?

Man is a being whom Allah furnishes with the faculty of thought. Yet, most people do not use this very important faculty as they should. In fact, some people almost never think.

In truth, each person possesses a capacity for thought of which even he himself is unaware. Once man begins to use this capacity, facts he has not been able to realise until that very moment begin to be uncovered for him. The deeper he goes in reflection, the more his capacity to think

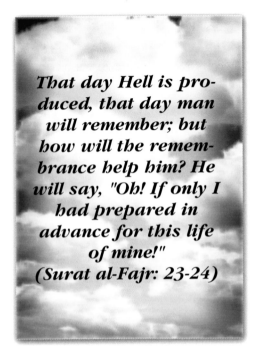

That day Hell is produced, that day man will remember; but how will the remembrance help him? He will say, "Oh! If only I had prepared in advance for this life of mine!" (Surat al-Fajr: 23-24)

improves, and this is possible for everyone. One just has to realise that one needs to reflect and then to strive hard.

The purpose of this book is to invite people to "think as they should" and show ways of "thinking as they should". Someone who does not think will remain totally distant from truths and lead his life in self-deception and error. As a result, he will not grasp the purpose of the creation of the world, and the reason for his existence on the earth. Yet, Allah has created everything with a purpose. This fact is stated in the Qur'an as follows:

We did not create the heavens and the earth and everything between them as a game. We did not create them except with truth but most of them do not know it. (Surat ad-Dukhan: 38-39) Did you suppose that We created you for amusement and that you would not return to Us? (Surat al-Muminun: 115)

Therefore, each person needs to ponder the purpose of creation, first as it concerns him himself, and then as it pertains to everything he sees in the universe and every event he experiences throughout his life. Someone who does not think, will understand the facts only after he dies, when he gives account before Allah, but then it will be too late. Allah says in the Qur'an that on the day of account, everybody will think and see the truth:

That day Hell is produced, that day man will remember; but how will the remembrance help him?
He will say, "Oh! If only I had prepared in advance for this life of mine!" (Surat al-Fajr: 23-24)

While Allah has given us a chance in the life of this world to reflect and derive conclusions from our reflections, to see the truth will bring us great gain in our life in the hereafter. For this reason, Allah has summoned all people, through His prophets and books, to reflect on their creation and on the creation of the universe:

Have they not reflected within themselves? Allah did not create the heavens and the earth and everything between them except with truth and for a fixed term. Yet many people reject the meeting with their Lord. (Surat ar-Rum: 8)

Deep Thinking

*M*ost people think that in order to "think deeply", one needs to put one's head between one's hands, withdraw to an empty room, and isolate oneself from all other people and affairs. Indeed, they make such a big thing of "thinking deeply" that they find it too difficult, and conclude that it is a quality exclusive to "philosophers".

However, as we stated in the introduction, Allah summons people to reflect and says that He has revealed the Qur'an for people to reflect on it: "It is a book We have sent down to you, full of blessing, so let people of intelligence **ponder** its signs and take heed." (Surah Sad: 29) What is important is one's sincerely improving one's ability to think and going deeper in thinking.

On the other hand, people who do not spend effort to that end continue their lives in deep "heedlessness". The word heedlessness has connotations like "neglectfulness without forgetting, abandoning, being mistaken, disregarding, being careless". The heedless state of those who do not reflect is a consequence of forgetting or deliberately disregarding the purpose of their creation and of the realities which religion teaches. Yet, this is an extremely dangerous course that may lead to hell. Correspondingly, Allah has warned people against being among the heedless:

Remember your Lord in yourself humbly and fearfully, without loudness of voice, morning and evening. Do not be of the heedless ones. (Surat al-A'raf: 205)
Warn them of the day of bitter regret when the affair will be resolved. But they take no notice and they do not believe. (Surah Maryam: 39)

In the Qur'an, Allah refers to people who reflect and who, after reflecting conscientiously, see the truth and therefore fear Him. Allah says that those who blindly follow their fathers without thinking, out of tradition, are wrong. When asked, these people say that they are religious and believe in Allah, yet, since they do not think, they do not amend their conduct from fear of Allah. In the following verses, the mentality of these people is clearly laid out:

Say: "To whom does the earth belong, and everyone in it, if you
have any knowledge?"
They will say: "To Allah." Say: "So will you not pay heed?"
Say: "Who is the Lord of the Seven Heavens and the Lord of the
Mighty Throne?"
They will say: "Allah." Say: "So will you not have taqwa?"
(Taqwa: Awe or fear of Allah, which inspires a person to be on guard against
wrong action and eager for actions which please Him.)
Say: "In whose hand is the dominion over everything, He who
gives protection and from whom no protection can be given, if
you have any knowledge?"
They will say: "Allah's." Say: "So how have you been bewitched?"
The fact is that We have given them the truth and they are liars.
(Surat al-Muminun: 84-90)

Thinking Removes the Spell on People

In the above verse, Allah asks people, "So how have you been
bewitched?" The word "bewitched" in the verse implies a state of mental
numbness that takes control of people as a whole. An unthinking person's
mind is benumbed, his sight becomes fuzzy, he acts as if he does not see
the facts before his eyes, and his faculty of judgement weakens. He
becomes incapable of grasping even a plain truth. He cannot be fully conscious of extraordinary events taking place right beside him. He does not
notice the intricate details of events. The reason for people's leading heedless lives for thousands of years and their staying away from thought as a
whole, as if it is merely a cultural heritage, is actually this mental numbness.

We can explain one of the outcomes of this collective spell with an
example:

Beneath the earth's surface lies a "boiling stratum" called magma. The
crust of the earth is very thin, which implies that this blaze is very close to
us, almost under our feet. In order to have a better understanding of how
thin the earth's crust is we can make a comparison: the thickness of the
earth's crust in proportion to the whole earth can be compared to the

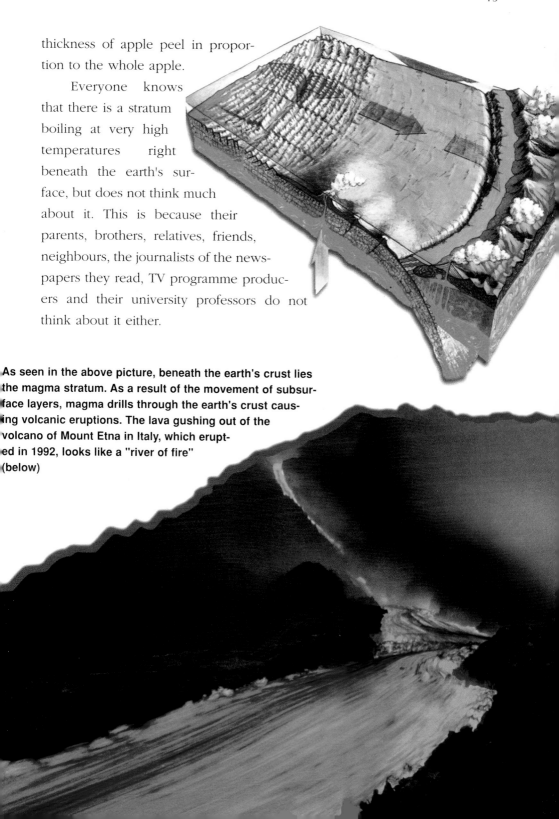

thickness of apple peel in proportion to the whole apple.

Everyone knows
that there is a stratum
boiling at very high
temperatures right
beneath the earth's sur-
face, but does not think much
about it. This is because their
parents, brothers, relatives, friends,
neighbours, the journalists of the newspapers they read, TV programme produc-
ers and their university professors do not
think about it either.

As seen in the above picture, beneath the earth's crust lies
the magma stratum. As a result of the movement of subsur-
face layers, magma drills through the earth's crust causing volcanic eruptions. The lava gushing out of the
volcano of Mount Etna in Italy, which erupt-
ed in 1992, looks like a "river of fire"
(below)

Let us try to make you think over this a little. Let us assume that a person, having lost his memory, tries to learn about his surroundings by asking questions of everyone around him. This person would first ask where he is. What would he think if he was told that beneath the ground he stands on lies a globe of boiling fire and that these flames could gush out of the earth's surface in the event of a strong earthquake or a volcanic eruption? Let us go further and suppose that this person was told that this world is simply a small planet and it floats in an infinite dark void called space and that space contains even greater dangers than the substratum of the earth. For example, meteors weighing tons freely move around in it. There is no reason why they should not alter their courses, perhaps because of some gravitational influence from another planet, and collide with the earth.

Surely, that person would not be able to forget, even for a moment, the risky situation he is in. He would investigate how people lead their lives in such an environment to which they hang on by the skin of their teeth. He would realise that a flawless system has been brought into being. The inside of the planet on which he lives contains great danger, yet very delicate balances prevent this danger from harming people, except in unusual circumstances. The person who realises this understands that the earth and all creatures on it live and continue their existence in safety only by the will of Allah, owing to the flawless balance He has created.

This example is only one of millions, even billions of examples upon which people need to ponder. Giving another example will be useful to help us understand how heedlessness affects people's faculty of thought and restrains their intellectual capacity.

People know that the life of this world passes away and ends very rapidly, yet still, they behave as if they will never leave this world. They act as if there is no death in the world. This, indeed, is a kind of "spell" carried over from generation to generation. This has such a strong effect that when someone talks about death, people immediately close the subject for fear of breaking the spell on them and facing the realities. People who have spent their entire lives in order to buy fine houses, summer residences and cars, and to send their children to good colleges, do not want to think that one day they will die and that they will not be able to take their cars, their houses, or children with them. Consequently, rather than beginning to do something for the real life after death, they choose not to think.

However, everyone, sooner or later, will definitely die and after one dies, whether one believes it or not, the eternal life will begin for everyone. Whether this eternal life will be spent in paradise or in hell depends on what one has done in the short life of this world. While such is the plain truth, the only reason why people behave as if death does not exist is this spell that has covered them up because they do not think.

Those who cannot, by thinking, save themselves from this spell and therefore from a heedless state, will understand the facts by seeing them with their eyes after they die. Allah communicates this fact in the Qur'an:

You were heedless of this, so We have stripped you of your covering and today your sight is sharp. (Surah Qaf: 22)

As Allah says in the verse, the sight which here is blurred because of not thinking, will be "sharp" at the time when the person gives account in the hereafter after death.

It should be pointed out that people deliberately impose on themselves such a spell. They suppose that by doing so they will live restful and relaxed lives. However, it is very easy for anyone to make a decision and shake off this mental numbness, and begin to live with a clear consciousness. Allah has presented the solution to people; people who reflect can dispel this enchantment while they are in the world. They thus come to understand that all events have a purpose and an inner meaning, and are able to see wisdom in the events that Allah creates at every instant.

Such a crowd makes one reflect upon Allah's unique vast creation. Since the moment the world came into existence, Allah has created billions of human faces, all different from each other.

One can Think at Anytime and Anywhere

There is no time, place or condition necessary for thought. Anyone may think while walking on the street, going to the office, driving a car, working at the computer, attending a friend's gathering, watching TV or having lunch.

While driving a car, for example, it is possible to see hundreds of people outdoors. He who looks at these people can think about many different things. It may come to his mind that the physical appearances of these hundreds of people are completely different. None of these people look like one another. It is astonishing that, although these people share basically similar organs such as eyes, eyebrows, eyelashes, hands, arms, legs, mouths and noses, they all look so different from one another. Thinking a little further, one remembers the following:

Allah has created billions of people over thousands of years all different from one another. This certainly is a piece of evidence of what a superior and mighty Creator Allah is.

The person watching all these people rushing may be occupied by many different thoughts. At first glance, each one of these people seems like a "distinct" individual. Every one of them has his own world, wishes, plans, ways of living, topics that make him happy or unhappy, and tastes. Yet these differences are misleading. In general, every human being is born, grows up, goes to school, looks for a job, works, marries, has children, sends the children to school, marries them off, ages, becomes a grandmother or grandfather and finally passes

Every self will taste death. You will be paid your wages in full on the Day of Rising. Anyone who is distanced from the Fire and admitted to the Garden has triumphed. The life of this world is just the enjoyment of delusion.
(Surat Al 'Imran: 185)

away. From this point of view, there are no big differences between people's lives. Whether one lives in a neighbourhood in Istanbul or in a Mexican city does not change anything at all. All of these people will definitely die one day. A century later, perhaps not even one of these people will be alive. The person who realises all this, carries on thinking and asks himself the following questions: "Since all of us will die one day, why do everybody act as if they will never depart from this world? While a person, whose death is certain, ought to strive for his life after death, how is it that almost all people behave as if their lives in this world will never end?"

Such a person is one who thinks and reaches a very crucial conclusion from what he thinks.

A great majority of people do not think about these issues. If they are suddenly asked, "what are you thinking at the moment?" it will be seen that they think extremely unnecessary things that will not be of much use to them. However, man is able to"think" "meaningful", "wise" and "important" subjects every moment from the time he wakes up until he sleeps, and derive conclusions from what he thinks.

In the Qur'an, Allah informs us that in all circumstances the believers reflect and derive beneficial conclusions from their thinking.

In the creation of the heavens and the earth and the alternation of night and day, there are signs for people with intelligence: those who remember Allah, standing, sitting and lying on their sides, and reflect on the creation of the heavens and the earth: "Our Lord, You have not created this for nothing. Glory be to You! So safeguard us from the punishment of the Fire." (Surat Al 'Imran: 190-191)

As we are also informed in the verse, because believers are people who reflect, they are able to see the miraculous side of the creation and exalt the power, knowledge and wisdom of Allah.

Thinking Sincerely by Turning Towards Allah

In order for contemplation to benefit a person and lead him to the right conclusion, he should always think positively. For instance, a person who – seeing someone far more handsome than himself – feels inferior because of his physical inadequacy by thinking about the other person's good looks or who becomes jealous of this person, is thinking a thought of which Allah does not approve. Yet, a person who aims to earn the approval of Allah considers the good looks of the other person as a manifestation of Allah's perfect creation. Since he looks at this person as a beauty Allah has created, he derives great pleasure from it. He asks Allah to enhance the beauty of this person in the hereafter. As for himself, he also asks Allah for true and eternal beauty in the hereafter. He realises that man can never be perfect in this world, because the world has been created with imperfections as a part of a test. His craving for paradise increases. This is certainly only one example of sincere thought. Throughout life, man encounters many instances like this. He is tested to see whether he displays good manners and a way of thought with which Allah will be pleased.

His being successful in the test and his contemplation bringing favour to him in the hereafter depend on his deriving lessons and warnings from the things on which he reflects. For this, it is imperative that one thinks truthfully continually. Allah states in the Qur'an:

It is He Who shows you His signs, and sends down provision to you out of heaven. But none pay heed save those who turn unto Him repentant. (Surah Ghafir: 13)

What Do People Usually Think About?

*J*n previous chapters, we mentioned that people do not think as they ought and do not develop their faculty of thinking. Yet here there is an important point that needs to be clarified. Surely certain things cross one's mind every moment of one's life. There is almost no moment, save at times of sleep, that the human mind is utterly blank. However, a great many of these are useless, "futile" and "unnecessary" thoughts that are of no avail in one's hereafter, that lead nowhere, and serve one no good.

If someone tries to remember what he thought during the day and notes it down, then looks over it at the end of the day, he would see how futile are most of his thoughts. Even if he were to find some of it useful, he would most likely be mistaken. For, on the whole, thoughts that seem correct may not be of any use in the hereafter.

Just as people waste time dealing with futile things in their daily lives, equally they spend time in vain carried away with futile thoughts. In the verse "Successful indeed are the believers...who keep aloof from what is vain..." (Surat al-Muminun: 3), Allah advises people to be strong-willed in this area. Surely, this command of Allah holds true for people's thoughts as well. This is because thoughts, unless we control them consciously, continuously flow through our minds. One unconsciously jumps from one thought to another. While thinking about the shopping one will purchase on one's way home, all of a sudden one finds oneself thinking about the things a friend told one two years ago. This uncontrolled and useless thinking may go on uninterruptedly throughout the day.

Yet controlling thought is possible. Everyone possesses the ability to think things that will improve him, his faith, mind, courtesy and his surroundings.

In this chapter, we will mention what sorts of things heedless people tend to think about in general. The reason these subjects are told in detail is so that people who read this book may realise immediately, when something similar to what is mentioned here crosses their minds as they go to work or school or while doing something casual, that they are thinking something useless. Therefore they might take their thoughts under control and think things that are truly useful for them.

Useless Worries

When one fails to control one's thoughts and direct them towards achieving a good end, one may often feel apprehension or treat events that have not happened as if they have occurred and become led astray by grief, distress, worry and fear.

Someone who has a young person studying for a university exam, for example, may make up scenarios before the exam takes place of what might happen in the case that his child fails the exam. "If, in the future, my son cannot find a good job and earn enough money, he will not be able to marry. Even if he marries, how will he be able to afford the expenses of a wedding? If he fails the exam, all the money spent on the preparatory courses will have been wasted and, moreover, we will be disgraced in the eyes of people. What if my best friend's son passes and my own son fails...?"

These misapprehensions go on and on. This person's son, however, has not even taken the examination yet. Throughout his life, someone who is distant from the religion cannot resist such useless worries. There is surely a reason for it. In the Qur'an, it has been related that the reason why people cannot be relieved of useless anxieties is their lending ear to the whisperings of satan:

(Satan:) "Most certainly I will lead them astray and excite in them vain desires..." (Surat an-Nisa: 119)

As seen in the above verse, he who is occupied with futile anxieties, who forgets Allah and does not think clearly, is always open to the whisperings of satan. In other words, if man, deceived by the life of the world, does not exercise his will-power and act conscientiously and if he lets himself drift in the course of events, he comes completely under the control of satan. One of the most crucial patterns of behaviour of satan is his giving people anxieties. Therefore, all misapprehensions, pessimism and anxieties such as "what will I do if such-and-such happens" contrived in the mind are caused by the whisperings of satan.

Allah shows people the way to save themselves from this situation. In the Qur'an, Allah advises people that when an evil impulse from satan provokes them, they should seek refuge in Allah and remember Him:

As for those who have taqwa, when they are bothered by visitors from Satan, they remember and immediately see clearly. But as for their brothers, the visitors lead them further into error. And they do not stop at that! (Surat al-A'raf: 201-202)

As stated in the verse, someone who reflects sees what is right, and someone who does not goes wherever satan drags him.

The important thing is to know that these thoughts will be of no use to the person and will, on the contrary, hamper him from thinking the truth, reflecting on important matters, and therefore purifying the mind from these useless thoughts. Man can think properly only if he frees his mind from futile thoughts. In this way, he "keeps aloof from what is vain" as Allah commands in the Qur'an.

What are the Reasons that Prevent Thought?

*T*here are many factors that hinder people from thinking. A single one, or a number, or all of them may detain a person from thinking and seeing the truth. In this respect, it is necessary that everyone identify the factors that affect them negatively, and be rid of them. Otherwise, one cannot see the real face of the life of this world, and that might bring great loss in the hereafter.

In the Qur'an, Allah tells us the situation of those people who are accustomed to think superficially:

They know an outward aspect of the life of this world but are heedless of the hereafter. Have they not reflected within themselves? Allah did not create the heavens and the earth and everything between them except with truth and for a fixed term. Yet many people reject the meeting with their Lord. (Surat ar-Rum: 7-8)

Following the Majority Causes Mental Numbness

One of the issues that mislead people most is their belief that what the "majority" does is right. Man is usually inclined to accept what he is taught by the people around him, rather than finding the truth by thinking. He sees that things that seem odd to him at first sight are most of the time considered ordinary by people, and moreover are not even noticed by them, and after a while, he too begins to become accustomed to them.

For instance, a great part of the people in his circle does not acknowledge that they will die one day. They do not even let anybody talk about this topic in order not to remember death. Seeing this, the person looks around him and says, "Since everybody is like that, there must be nothing wrong with my behaving the same way" and begins to live without remembering death at all. If, however, the people around him had acted with fear of Allah and struggled with due struggle for the hereafter, most probably this person too would have changed his attitude.

As another example, on TVs and magazines, hundreds of news items of disasters, unfairness, injustice, oppression, suicide, homicide, theft and swindle are covered, and thousands of needy people are mentioned everyday. Yet many people who read these news items turn the pages of the newspaper or switch the TV channels with inner calm. In general, people do not think why there are so many of these kind of news items, or what has to be done and what kind of precautions have to be taken in order to stop them, or what they themselves can do about these problems. Neither do people around them think over those problems. Most people hold others responsible for these problems, employing such logic as "is it up to me to save the world?"

Mental Indolence

Indolence is a factor that keeps the majority of people from thinking. Because of mental indolence, people do everything the way they have always seen and to which they are used. To give an example from our daily lives, the way housewives do the cleaning is just how they have seen their mothers do it. They generally do not think, "how could things be done in a cleaner and more practical way" nor try to find new methods. Similarly, when something needs repair, men use the methods they have been taught since their childhood. They are generally reluctant to practise a new method that might be more practical and efficient. Such people's styles of speech are also the same. The way an accountant speaks, for example, is just the same as all the other accountants he has seen in his life. Doctors, bankers, salesmen... people from all classes have particular styles of speech. They do not seek to find the most proper, the best, and the most favourable way by thinking about it. They just imitate what they have heard.

The solutions found to problems also reflect indolence in thinking. For example, the manager of a building brings to the building's garbage problem exactly the same solution as the one brought by previous managers. Or a mayor tries to solve the traffic problem by looking at what preceding mayors have done. In many cases, because of not thinking he is unable to find new solutions.

Certainly, the examples cited here are issues from which people suffer harm in their everyday lives. Yet there are subjects far more important than those, which, if people fail to think about, may cause them to suffer great and eternal loss. The cause of this loss is one's failure to think about the purpose of existence in the world, and disregarding the fact that death is unavoidable, and that we will definitely meet the day of reckoning after death. In the Qur'an, Allah invites people to reflect upon these crucial matters.

Those are the people who have lost their own selves. What they invented has abandoned them. Without question they will be the greatest losers in the hereafter. As for those who believe and do right actions and humble themselves before their Lord, they are the Companions of the Garden, remaining in it timelessly, forever. The likeness of the two groups is that of the blind and deaf and the seeing and hearing. Are they the same as one another? So will you not pay heed? (Surah Hud: 21-24)
Is He Who creates like him who does not create? So will you not pay heed? (Surat an-Nahl: 17)

The Conditioned Response that "Thinking Too Much is Not Good"

There is a conviction prevalent in society that deep thought is not good. People warn one another saying "don't think so much, you will lose your mind". This is surely nothing but a superstition invented by people who are remote from religion. People should not avoid thinking but thinking negatively or being carried away by exaggerated scruples and misapprehensions.

Since those who don't have strong faith in Allah and the hereafter think without committing themselves to goodness, but instead negatively, then by their contemplation they achieve outcomes that are not entirely beneficial. They think, for example, that the life of this world is temporary, and that one-day they will die, but this causes them to display great pessimism. This is because, conscientiously, they are aware that the life they pass without following the commands of Allah prepares a wretched end for them in the hereafter. Some, on the other hand, are pessimistic because they believe that they will totally vanish after death.

A wise person who believes in Allah and the hereafter draws completely different conclusions when he reflects on the fact that the life of this world is temporary. First of all, his realisation that the world is temporary causes him to engage in zealous struggle for his real and eternal life in the hereafter. Since he knows that this life will sooner or later end, he does not become carried away by the ambition for worldly passions and interests. He is extremely resigned. Nothing in this temporary life annoys him. He always cherishes the hope of attaining an eternal and pleasant life. He also greatly enjoys worldly blessings and beauty. Allah has created the world incomplete and flawed in order to test people. The intelligent person thinks that if there is so much beauty, which is pleasing to man even in this incomplete and flawed world, then the beauty of paradise should be unimaginably more attractive. He hopes to see in the hereafter the "originals" of every beauty he views here. And he comprehends all of these by thinking deeply.

Therefore, it would be a great loss to worry about "what if I become pessimistic by finally seeing the truth", and hence, avoid thinking. For a person who always entertains hope by virtue of his faith in Allah, and who thinks positively, there is nothing that leads to pessimism.

Avoiding the Responsibilities that Thinking Brings

Most people think that they might be able to evade various responsibilities by avoiding thinking and setting their brain to work on certain issues. By doing so in the world, they succeed in holding themselves aloof from many subjects. One of the greatest ways in which people are deceived, however, is in their supposition that they can escape their responsibilities to their Lord by not thinking. This is the main reason why people do not think about death and life after death. If man thinks that he will die one day and remembers that there is an eternal life after death, he will necessarily have to strive strenuously for his life after death. He, however, deceives himself, supposing that he is saved from such responsibility when he does not think of the existence of the hereafter. This is a great self-deception, and if man does not attain the truth in this world by think-ing, he will understand, with death, that there is no escape for him.

**The stupor of death will come in truth. (And it is said unto him):
"That is what you were trying to evade! The trumpet is blown.
That is the day of the threat." (Surah Qaf: 19-20)**

Not Thinking Because of Being Swept Away by the Flow of Daily Life

The majority of people spend their whole lives in a "rush". When they reach a certain age, they have to work and look after themselves and their families. They call this "the struggle for life" and complain that they have no time for anything as they have to rush around in this struggle. In this

**One of the most important factors that hinder men from deep thought
is the overload of their daily affairs.**

so-called "shortage of time", thinking is one of the things for which they cannot spare any time. Therefore, they are swept away wherever the flow of their daily lives takes them. In this way of life, they become insensitive to events taking place around them.

The aim of man, however, should not be to consume time, rushing from one place to another. The main issue is to be able to see the real face of this world and assume a way of living accordingly. No one's sole purpose is earning money, going to work, studying at university or purchasing a house. Surely, man may need to do those things in the course of his life, yet there is a subject that he should always bear in mind while doing them: the purpose of his existence in this world is to be a slave of Allah, to work for Allah's pleasure, His mercy and paradise. All works other than this purpose can serve only as a "means" helping man to attain his true purpose. Adopting the means to certain ends as the real purposes is a serious deception with which satan misleads man.

Someone who lives without thinking may easily take these means as his real purpose. We can cite an example from our daily lives. It is undoubtedly a good act for one to work and produce beneficial things for society. A person who believes in Allah performs such an act eagerly and expects a reward from Allah both in the world and in the hereafter. If a person, on the other hand, does the same thing without remembering Allah and only for worldly interests such as status and people's appreciation, he is making a mistake. He has made something, which he should use as a means of earning the pleasure of Allah, his purpose. And he will regret this when he faces realities in the hereafter. In a verse, Allah refers to those who indulge in this manner in the life of this world as follows:

Like those before you who had greater strength than you and more wealth and children. They enjoyed their portion; so enjoy your portion as those before you enjoyed theirs. You have plunged into defamation as they plunged into it. The actions of such people come to nothing in this world or the hereafter. They are the lost. (Surat at-Tawba: 69)

Looking at Everything with "The Eye of Habit" And Therefore Seeing No Need to Reflect Thereon

When people come across certain things for the first time, they may understand the extraordinary nature of them and this may spur them to further inspect what they see. After a while, however, they develop a habitual resistance to those things and they no longer impress them. In particular, an object or happening they meet everyday becomes "ordinary" for them.

For instance, it makes a great impression on some prospective doctors the first time they see a corpse, or the first time one of their patients dies. This makes them ponder deeply. It may be that all of a sudden they face the lifeless, almost stuff-like body of a person, who was, just a few minutes ago, full of life, laughing, making plans, talking, taking pleasure, eyes sparkling with life. The first time a cadaver is laid down in front of them for autopsy, they think over everything they see in that corpse: that the body decays so fast, that a repugnant smell comes out of it, that the hair once so pleasant to look at become so unpleasant that one doesn't want to touch it, are all subjects they think about. After those they think this: the composition of everyone's body is the same and everyone will meet the same end, that is, they too will become like this.

Yet, after seeing a couple of cadavers or losing a couple of patients, these people develop a habitual resistance to certain things. They begin to treat cadavers, and even patients, as if they are objects.

Surely, this situation does not hold true for doctors alone. For the majority of people, the same situation applies in many areas of their lives. For example, when a person who lives in difficulty is granted a pleasant life-style, he understands that everything he possesses is a blessing for him. That his bed is more comfortable, his house has a beautiful view, he can buy everything he wants, he can heat his house in winter as he wishes, he can easily move by car, and many other things are all blessings for this person. Thinking of his old state, he rejoices at each of these. Yet someone who possesses these means from birth may not think so much about their worth. So, his appreciation of these blessings does not become possible unless he thinks over them.

For a man who ponders, on the other hand, it makes no difference whether he possesses these blessings from birth or attained them afterwards. He never looks at his possessions in a habitual way. He knows that anything he owns has been created by Allah and Allah may take them back from him if He wills. For example, believers say the following prayer when they mount their riding beasts, that is, their vehicles:

So that you might sit firmly on their backs and remember your Lord's blessing while you are seated on them, saying, "Glory be to Him who has subjected this to us. We could never have done it by ourselves. Indeed we are returning to our Lord!" (Surat az-Zukhruf: 13-14)

In another verse, it is said that when believers enter their gardens, they remember Allah and say, **"It is as Allah wills, there is no strength but in Allah"** (Surat al-Kahf: 39). Whenever they enter their gardens, they think that Allah has created and sustains this garden. On the other hand, a man who does not think may be impressed the first time he sees a beautiful garden, but then it becomes an ordinary place for him. His admiration fades for the beauty therein. Some people do not realise these blessings at all since they do not think. They take these blessings as "usual" and "something that already had to exist". Therefore, they cannot derive pleasure from their beauty.

Conclusion: It is Imperative for Man to Eliminate All the Factors That Hold Him Back From Thinking

As we said earlier, that the majority of people do not think and live heedless of truth cannot be sufficient excuse for one not thinking. Each person is an independent individual responsible to Allah by himself alone. It is very important to bear in mind that Allah tests people in the life of this world. The indifference of others, their being people who do not think, reason, and see the truth is, most of the time, a part of this test. A person who thinks sincerely does not say "most of the people do not reflect, and are unaware of all these, so why should I alone think?" On the contrary, he takes warning by thinking about the heedlessness of these people, and takes refuge in Allah in order not be one of them. It is clear that the situation of these people cannot be an excuse for him. In the Qur'an, Allah informs us in many of His verses that most people are heedless and do not believe:

Yet no faith will the greater part of mankind have, however ardently you desire it. (Surah Yusuf: 103)

Alif Lam Mim Ra. Those are the signs of the Book. And what has been sent down to you from your Lord is the truth. But most people do not believe. (Surat ar-Ra'd: 1)

They swear by Allah with their most earnest oaths that Allah will not raise up those who die, when, on the contrary, it is a binding promise on Him; but most people do not know it. (Surat an-Nahl: 38)

We have variegated it for them so they might pay heed but most people begrudge aught save ingratitude. (Surat al-Furqan: 50)

In other verse, Allah announces the end of those who have gone astray by following the majority, failed to obey the commands of Allah by forgetting the purpose of their creation:

They will shout out in it, "Our Lord! Take us out! We will act rightly, differently from the way we used to act!" Did We not let you live long enough for anyone who was going to pay heed to pay heed? And did not the warner come to you? Taste it then! There is no helper for the wrongdoers. (Surah Fatir: 37)

For this reason, every person should, by getting rid of the reasons preventing him from thinking, sincerely and honestly think over every event and creature that Allah creates and draw a lesson and warning from his reflections.

In the next chapter, we will be discussing what man may reflect on about certain events and creatures he may come across in his daily life. Our purpose is to have these subjects provide the readers of this book with a guidance and help them spend the rest of their lives as people who "think and draw warnings from what they reflect on".

Those Things
that Need to be
Thought About

*F*rom the beginning of the book, we referred to the importance of thinking, the gains it brings man and that thought is a very important faculty that separates man from other creatures. We also mentioned the causes that prevent thinking. The main purpose in all this was to encourage people to think and to help them see the purpose of their creation and honour Allah's endless knowledge and might.

In the following pages, we will try to describe what a person believing in Allah would think about the things he meets during the day, what lessons he would draw from the events he witnesses, how he should thank and come closer to Allah by seeing his Lord's art and knowledge in everything.

Certainly what will be mentioned here covers only a very small part of a man's thinking capacity. Man has the ability to think every moment (not hour, minute, or second but moment) of his life. The scope of man's thought is so broad that it is almost not possible to put any constraints or limits on it. The purpose of what will be told below is only to open a door for people who do not make use of their faculty of thinking as is appropriate.

It should be born in mind that only people who reflect can understand and assume a different position than others. The situation of those who cannot see the miraculous events around them and cannot reflect has been related in the verses of Allah as follows:

The likeness of those who disbelieve is that of someone who yells out to something which cannot hear – it is nothing but a cry and a call. Deaf – dumb – blind. They do not use their intellects. (Surat al-Baqara: 171)

...They have hearts they do not understand with. They have eyes they do not see with. They have ears they do not hear with. Such people are like cattle. No, they are even further astray! They are the unaware. (Surat al-A'raf: 179)

Do you suppose that most of them hear or understand? They are just like cattle. Indeed they are even more astray! (Surat al-Furqan: 44)

Those who are able to see Allah's signs, the miraculous aspects of the beings and events He creates, and who, therefore, can understand, are people who reflect. Such people can derive conclusions from everything, big or small, they see around them.

When One Wakes up in the Morning...

There is no need for special conditions for someone to start thinking. From the moment we wake up in the morning, plenty of opportunities for thought lie before us.

A long day lies before us when we wake up in the morning. Most of the time, we do not feel tired or sleepless, we are ready to start everything over again. Thinking this, one remembers a verse of Allah:

It is He who made the night a cloak for you and sleep a rest, and He made the day a time for rising. (Surat al-Furqan: 47)

Washing the face and taking a shower, we pull ourselves together and come more fully to our senses. Now we are ready to think on many useful issues. There are many concerns much more important than what we will have for breakfast or what time we have to leave home, and we first have to think about them.

First of all, our being able to wake up in the morning is a great miracle. Despite having lost consciousness entirely, in the morning we recover consciousness and our personalities. The heart beats, we are able to breathe, talk and see. In fact, when we go to sleep, there is no guarantee that these favours will be returned to us in the morning. Nor have we met any disasters during the night. For example, the absent-mindedness of a neighbour could cause a gas leakage and great explosion during the night could have woken us. A catastrophe could have occurred in the region where we lived and we could have lost our lives.

We could have had other problems with our bodies; for example, we could have woken up with severe pains in the kidneys or with a headache. Yet, none of these happened and we have woken up safe and sound. Thinking on all of this, we thank Allah for His mercy and protection.

Starting a new day in good health means Allah's giving us another chance to achieve more for the hereafter.

Therefore, the best attitude to take is that we will spend our day in such a way as to please Allah. Man should, prior to everything else, make plans for this and keep his mind occupied with thoughts of that sort. The starting point for pleasing Allah is to ask Him for help about this matter. The prayer of the prophet Sulayman sets a good example for the believers:

...My Lord, keep me thankful for the blessing You have bestowed on me and on my parents, and keep me acting rightly, pleasing You, and admit me, by Your mercy, among Your righteous slaves. (Surat an-Naml: 19)

What Our Weaknesses Make Us Think

Realising our incapacities as soon as we get out of our beds, we start to think. Every morning we definitely have to wash our faces and brush our teeth. Seeing these, we start to think of our other weaknesses. For instance, that we have to take a bath every day, that under our thin skin there is such a terrible sight, that our bodies are extremely open to infections, and cannot stand sleeplessness, hunger and thirst. These are all signs of our weakness.

If the person looking in the mirror in the morning is aged, some other thoughts may come to mind. The first signs of ageing start to appear in the face after the first two decades of life. In the thirties, wrinkles begin to appear beneath the eyes and around the mouth; the skin is no longer as ruddy as it used to be, and deterioration can be observed in a great part of the body. With age, the hair turns white, and even the hands age.

It is Allah who created you from a weak beginning then after weakness gave you strength then after strength ordained weakness and grey hair. He creates whatever He wills. He is All-Knowing, All-Powerful. (Surat ar-Rum: 19)

For someone who thinks about these, old age is one of the most powerful events displaying the temporary nature of the life of this world, and it holds one back from being attached greedily to this world. Someone who starts to grow old understands that a countdown has started in his life in this world. In truth, that which ages and for which the countdown is now underway is the body. The body gradually declines but the soul does not grow old. Most people are strongly influenced by the fact of their being good looking or unattractive in their youth. In general, people who used to be good-looking are often arrogant where people who used to be unattractive feel inferior and unhappy. Ageing shows how temporary the body's beauty or ugliness is, that the only thing that is acceptable before Allah and the only gain of man are right actions, good qualities of character along with commitment to Allah.

Each time we face our weaknesses, we realise that the only being that is Perfect and High Exalted above imperfections is Allah, and then we glorify the greatness of Allah. Allah has created every weakness man possesses with a purpose. Some of these purposes are to help people not to be attached to the life of this world, and not go astray with their possessions. Someone who grasps these by thinking, wants Allah to recreate him in the hereafter free from all these weaknesses.

Our weaknesses remind us of another very important thought. While a rose growing up from the black soil smells perfectly clean, an unbearable smell emanates from us when we do not look after ourselves. This is something that arrogant and conceited people in particular have to think about and from which they should take warning.

A rose growing out of muddy, black soil smells perfectly clean.

What Some Features of the Human Body Make One Think About

Looking at the mirror in the morning, we may think about many things we have not thought about before. For example, our eyelashes, eyebrows, bones and teeth stop growing when they reach a certain length. However, hair does not stop growing. In other words, whereas those body

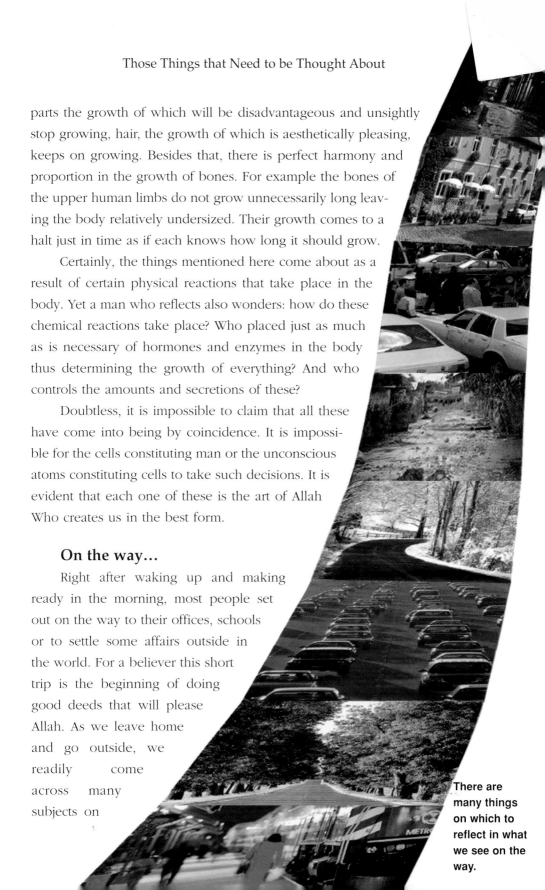

parts the growth of which will be disadvantageous and unsightly stop growing, hair, the growth of which is aesthetically pleasing, keeps on growing. Besides that, there is perfect harmony and proportion in the growth of bones. For example the bones of the upper human limbs do not grow unnecessarily long leaving the body relatively undersized. Their growth comes to a halt just in time as if each knows how long it should grow.

Certainly, the things mentioned here come about as a result of certain physical reactions that take place in the body. Yet a man who reflects also wonders: how do these chemical reactions take place? Who placed just as much as is necessary of hormones and enzymes in the body thus determining the growth of everything? And who controls the amounts and secretions of these?

Doubtless, it is impossible to claim that all these have come into being by coincidence. It is impossible for the cells constituting man or the unconscious atoms constituting cells to take such decisions. It is evident that each one of these is the art of Allah Who creates us in the best form.

On the way...

Right after waking up and making ready in the morning, most people set out on the way to their offices, schools or to settle some affairs outside in the world. For a believer this short trip is the beginning of doing good deeds that will please Allah. As we leave home and go outside, we readily come across many subjects on

There are many things on which to reflect in what we see on the way.

which we ought to reflect. There are thousands of people, cars, trees, big and small, and countless details all around us. Here, the outlook of a believer is very clear. We try to get the most from what we see around us. We think about the causes of events. The view we confront has come about within the knowledge of Allah and His will. Therefore, there should certainly be causes behind it. Since Allah made us go out, and set these images before us, there must be something to be seen in them and thought about. From the moment we wake up, we give thanks to Allah for having given us another day in this world to earn our reward with our Lord. Now, we have started a journey in which we can earn these rewards. Being aware of this, we think about the verse of Allah: **"We made the day for earning a living."** (Surat an-Naba': 11) In accordance with this verse, we make plans on how to spend the day in doing deeds that are useful to other people and with which Allah is pleased.

When we reach our car or any other vehicle with these plans in mind, we again give thanks to Allah. No matter how far the destination, we have the means to get there. As a convenience, Allah has created many vehicles

A person who thinks sees that it is Allah Who puts technology at the service of mankind.

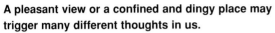
A pleasant view or a confined and dingy place may trigger many different thoughts in us.

for people to use in travel. In particular, recent technological developments have introduced many new possibilities such as cars, trains, aeroplanes, ships, helicopters, buses, etc. Pondering this, one remembers one more issue: it is Allah Who puts the technology at the service of mankind.

Everyday, scientists come up with new discoveries and innovations that facilitate our lives. They accomplish all these with the means that Allah creates on the earth. Someone who thinks, carries on his trip by giving thanks to his Lord for putting these at his service.

Heading towards our destination accompanied by such thoughts, a stack of rubbish, a foul odour, the confined, dingy places we see in between streets bring various thoughts to our minds.

In this world, Allah has created settings and sights by means of which we are able to visualise both paradise and hell, or guess, through comparison, how they will be. Stacks of rubbish, foul odours, confined, dingy and dark places cause considerable distress to our souls. One never wants to be in such places. All these qualities remind one of hell and anyone who meets such scenes remembers the verses about hell. Allah has depicted in many verses of the Qur'an the unpleasant sights, darkness, and filth of the hell:

And the Companions of the Left: what of the Companions of the Left? Amid searing blasts and scalding water,
And the murk of thick black smoke,
Providing no coolness and no pleasure. (Surat al-Waqi'a: 41-44)
When they are flung into a narrow place in it, shackled together in chains, they will cry out there for destruction. "Do not cry out today for just one destruction, cry out for many destructions!" (Surat al-Furqan: 13-14)

Remembering these ayat of the Qur'an, we pray to Allah for Him to protect us from the fury of hell and we ask forgiveness for our mistakes.

One who does not employ such modes of thought, on the other hand, spends his day grumbling, fussing, and looking for the offender in every incident. He will become furious at people who dump their garbage and at the municipality that was late to collect it. He will busy his mind with many subjects throughout the day such as holes in the roads, those who block the traffic, his becoming soaked due to a wrong weather forecast by the meteorologists, and finally the unjust scolding he receives from his boss. These vain thoughts, however, are of no use to him in his afterlife. One might stop to think whether he should push so many things aside. Indeed, many people claim the real reason that keeps them from thinking is the struggle they have to carry on in this world. They say that they cannot think because of problems such as food, accommodation and health. This, however, is nothing but an excuse. One's responsibilities and the state one is in have nothing to do with one's thinking. Someone who tries to think to gain the pleasure of Allah will find Allah's help beside him. He will see that the issues that used to be a problem for him are solved one

by one and every passing day he will be able to spare more and more time to think. This is something understood and experienced only by believers.

What A Multi-Coloured World Makes One Think

Continuing on our journey, we try to see Allah's signs and creational miracles around us, and honour our Lord's glory by thinking about them. When we look out from the car window, we see a multi-coloured world. We then think: "What would everything be like if the world were not multi-coloured?"

Have a look at the pictures below and think. Would we derive the same pleasure as we now do from a sea or mountain landscape or a flower without colour? Would images of the sky, fruits, butterflies, clothes, and faces of people give us as much pleasure as they now do? It is a favour from our Lord that we live in a vibrant multi-coloured world. Every colour we see in nature, the perfect harmony of living beings' colours are all signs of the matchless art and unique creation of Allah. The colours of a flower, or a bird and the harmony of these colours or the soft interplay between colours, the fact that nothing disturbs our eyes in nature, that, for instance,

the colours of the seas, the sky, and the trees are in tones that give us peace and do not exhaust our eyes, show the perfection of Allah's creation. Reflecting on all these, we come to understand that everything we see around us is a work of the infinite knowledge and omnipotence of Allah. In return for all these favours Allah has granted us, we fear Allah and seek His protection from being ungrateful. In the Qur'an, Allah reminds us of the presence of colours, and states that only those who have knowledge have fear of Allah. Elsewhere, Allah makes it clear that the believers continually reflect and use their intellects, explore by thinking and derive conclusions from their reflections:

Do you not see that Allah sends down water from the sky and by it We bring forth fruits of varying colours? And in the mountains there are streaks of white and red, or varying shades, and rocks of deep jet black. And mankind and beasts and livestock are likewise of varying colours. Only those of His slaves with knowledge have fear of Allah. Allah is Almighty, Ever-Forgiving. (Surah Fatir: 27-28)

What A Hearse Seen on the Way Should Make One Think

A person who rushes to his destination may suddenly run into a hearse. In fact, this is a very important opportunity for someone to pull himself together. The sight he meets reminds him of death. One day, he, too, will be in that hearse. There is no doubt about it, no matter how much he evades it, death will sooner or later find him. Whether in his bed, or on his way, or on vacation, he will certainly leave this world. For death is an unavoidable reality.

At that instant, a believer remembers the following verses of Allah:

Every self will taste death. Then you will be returned to Us. As for those who believe and do right actions, We will lodge them in lofty chambers in the Garden, with rivers flowing under them, remaining in them timelessly, for ever. How excellent is the reward of those who act: those who are steadfast and put their trust in their Lord. (Surat al-'Ankabut: 57-59)

Certainly, the consideration that his own body will also be placed in a shroud, covered with soil by his kinsmen, his forename and surname carved on a gravestone, removes man's attachment to the world. Someone who sincerely and realistically thinks about this, sees how senseless it is to lay claim to a body which one day is to decay in the earth.

In the verse of Surat al-'Ankabut, Allah gives the glad tidings of paradise after death to those who are patient and put their trust in Allah. For this reason, believers, thinking that they will die one day, try to live sincerely directed towards Allah, living in right action and with the good character commanded by Allah to attain paradise. Every time they think about the closeness of death, their determination grows and they try to adopt the highest values and increasingly develop them throughout their lives.

On the other hand, those who give precedence to other thoughts, and spend their lives in vain anxieties, do not think that the same will definitely befall them one day, even in the event that they come across a hearse and even though they pass by cemeteries every day, and even when some of their loved ones die besides them.

A funeral we encounter should make us think of "our own death" and that this world is short and temporary.

During the Day...

In the face of all events he comes across throughout the day, a believer always thinks of Allah's verses, and tries to have an understanding of the subtleties in events.

He reacts to each favour or trial with the good character of which Allah will approve. For a person who believes, the place he is in has little importance. Whether at school, at work, or shopping, by reflecting on the fact that Allah creates everything, he tries to see, the hidden purpose in events and the beauties that He creates, and he leads a life abiding by the verses of his Lord. This attitude of believers is related in the Qur'an as follows:

> **There are men who proclaim His glory morning and evening, not distracted by trade or commerce from the remembrance of Allah and the establishment of salat** (regular Prayer) **and the payment of zakat** (regular Charity)**; fearing a day when all hearts and eyes will be in turmoil – so that Allah can reward them for the best of what they did and give them more from His unbounded favour. Allah provides for anyone He wills without reckoning. (Surat an-Nur: 37-38)**

What Difficulties Someone Meets at Work Make Him Think

Man may encounter various difficulties throughout the day. However, whatever difficulty he encounters, he needs to put his trust in Allah and think as such: "Allah tests us with everything we do and we think about in the life of this world. This is a very important reality of which we should not lose sight even for a moment. Therefore, if we meet a difficulty in anything that we do or think that things do not proceed on the right track, we should never forget that all these events are set against us to test our conduct."

These thoughts which cross one's mind are true of all major or minor events one encounters during the day. For instance, we may make extra payments due to a misunderstanding or carelessness, we may lose a file

It is essential to think that there is good in all events that seem like trouble and then everything will result in the best way with the help of Allah.

on the computer on which we spent hours due to a powercut, a young student may fail in a university exam although he studied very hard, our days may pass waiting in queues about some work in progress due to bureaucratic procedures, work may go wrong because of missing documents, one may miss the plane or the bus on the way to somewhere one must reach very urgently... There are numerous such incidents which everyone may, and almost certainly will, come across in his lifetime and consider a difficulty and "trouble".

In all these incidents, a person with faith immediately thinks that Allah is testing his conduct and patience, and that it is senseless for a man who will die and give account in the hereafter to be carried away by such incidents and lose time by worrying about them. He knows that there is good behind all these events. He never says "Alas" to any happening and asks Allah to facilitate his work and turn everything to good purpose.

And when relief follows difficulty, we realise that this is an answer to our prayer to Allah, that Allah is the Hearer of prayers and He responds to them, and we give thanks to Allah.

Living through the day thinking these thoughts, one never becomes hopeless, worries, feels sorry, or is left desperate, no matter what one encounters. We know that Allah has created all of these for a good and that there is a blessing in them. Moreover, we think like this not only in major events that may befall us but, as we have mentioned, also in all of the details, big or small, we meet in our daily life.

Think of a man who cannot settle an important matter as he wishes, and who encounters serious problems just when he is about to reach his goal. This person suddenly becomes angry, feels unhappy and distressed and, in short, develops all sorts of negative feelings. However, someone who thinks that there is good in everything, tries to find the hidden purpose in this event which Allah shows him. He thinks that Allah may have brought to his attention that he must take more definite measures regarding this issue. He takes all the essential measures and gives thanks to Allah saying, "maybe this helped to prevent more serious harm."

Someone who misses the bus while trying to reach an appointment may think, "perhaps my being late and not being on this bus have saved me from an accident or another harm". These are only a few examples. One may also think, "there might be many other such hidden purposes". These kinds of examples can be multiplied within a man's life. The important thing is that our plans may not always be resolved according to our wishes. We may suddenly find ourselves in a completely different situation than we had planned. In such circumstances, someone who behaves resignedly and looks for good in the particular event he faces, prospers. Allah states in His verse:

It may be that you hate something when it is good for you and it may be that you love something when it is bad for you. Allah knows and you do not know. (Surat al-Baqara: 216)

As Allah states in His verse, we cannot know but Allah knows. Therefore, it is Allah Who knows what is good and bad for us. What falls to man is merely to take Allah, Full of Kindness and Most Merciful, for a friend and submit to Allah with full submission.

Things that are Thought While Working at Something...

It is important that while working on something, we do not let our minds go blank and that we always think of the good. The human mind is capable of doing more than one thing at a time. A person driving a car, cleaning the house, working, walking on the street, can also think of acts of goodness at the same time.

While cleaning the house, the person gives thanks to Allah for having given him such everyday means as water and detergents. Knowing that Allah loves cleanliness and clean people, he sees the work he does as an act of worship and with it hopes to earn the good pleasure of Allah. In addition, he takes pleasure in offering a comfortable setting for other people by cleaning the place in which he resides.

Someone working at a job prays to Allah in secret constantly, asks his Lord to facilitate his work, and thinks that he cannot succeed in anything unless Allah wills. We see that in the Qur'an, the prophets, who set an example for us, constantly turn towards Allah in secret, and think of Allah while working. One of these precious people is the prophet Musa. After helping two women he met on his way to water their flocks, he turned towards Allah with the following words:

When he arrived at the water of Madyan, he found a crowd of people drawing water there. Standing apart from them, he found two women, holding back their sheep. He said, "What are you two doing here?" They said, "We cannot draw water until the shepherds have driven off their sheep. You see our father is a very old man." So he drew water for them and then withdrew

into the shade and said, "My Lord, I am truly in need of any good You have in store for me." (Surat al-Qasas: 23-24)

Another example we see in the Qur'an about this subject is that of the prophets Ibrahim and Isma'il. Allah says that these prophets thought of good things for other believers while working together, and they turned towards Him and prayed to Him about their work:

And when Ibrahim built the foundations of the House with Isma'il: "Our Lord, accept this from us! You are the All-Hearing, the All-Knowing. Our Lord, make us both Muslims submitted to You, and our descendants a Muslim community submitted to You. Show us our rites of worship and turn towards us. You are the Ever-Returning, the Most Merciful. Our Lord, raise up among them a Messenger from them to recite Your Signs to them and teach them the Book and Wisdom and purify them. You are Almighty, the All-Wise." (Surat al-Baqara: 127-129)

What A Cobweb Makes One Think

There are many things to think for someone who spends his day at home. For example, while doing cleaning, he might see a spider that has woven its web in a corner of the house. If he realises that he ought to think about this creature which is normally of no importance to anyone, he will see new doors being opened for him. This tiny insect he sees before him is a miracle of design. There is perfect symmetry in the web the spider has woven. If, by any chance, he wonders how a tiny spider could achieve such astonishingly perfect design, and if he makes quick research, he will encounter some other extraordinary facts: the thread a spider uses is thirty percent more flexible than a rub-

There are many things in the perfect design of the web produced by a tiny insect on which to think.

ber thread of the same thickness. The thread the spider produces is of such a superior quality that men use it as a model for the manufacture of bullet-proof vests. Indeed, a substance, which many people consider a 'simple' spider's web, is in fact equivalent to one of the most ideal industrial materials of the world.

As man witnesses the perfect design of the living things around him, if he keeps on thinking, he will come across even more astonishing facts. When he examines the fly, which he constantly meets, but to which he has never paid attention, and at which he has even become angry and tried to kill, he sees that it has a very meticulous and detailed habit of cleaning itself. The fly frequently alights on a spot and cleans its fore- and hindlimbs separately. Then it cleans the dust off on its wings and head thoroughly with its fore- and hind-limbs. It continues cleaning until it is assured of its cleanliness. All other types of flies and insects clean themselves in a similar way, with the same attention to detail and meticulousness. This indicates that the Unique Creator taught them how to clean themselves.

The same fly flaps it wings approximately 500 times per second while flying. In fact, no man-made machine could operate at such a rate, but would shatter and burn because of friction. However, neither the wings, muscles, nor the joints of the fly are harmed. Taking into account the direction and speed of the wind, it can fly in any direction with-

There are many lessons in the fly cleaning itself.

out being diverted. Even with our current technology, man is very distant from producing a device with these extraordinary features and techniques of flight. Yet such an insignificant living being, which man brushes aside and pays no attention to, achieves something remarkable that man so far has been unable to achieve. Clearly, it is impossible to claim that a fly does this by merit of its abilities and intelligence. Allah has given the fly all its outstanding characteristics and abilities.

There is both visible and invisible life everywhere around us we casually glance. There is not even a square centimetre on the earth where life does not exist. Humans, plants, and animals are creatures that man is able to see, yet there are also creatures that man cannot see but of whose existence he is aware. The houses we live in, for example, are full of microscopic creatures called "mites". Similarly, in the air we breathe are countless viruses. The number of bacteria living in the soil of our gardens is astonishingly high.

The person who reflects on the incredibly diverse life of the earth also

That bees produce honey in as a cure for human illness, is a subject on which we need to reflect.

remembers the perfect systems of these creatures. All the creatures we see are each a clear sign of Allah's art. In the same manner, great miracles are hidden in microscopic creatures as well. The virus, bacterium or mite which are all invisible to us, have

Invisible mites

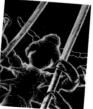

their own bodily mechanisms. Allah created their habitats, feeding patterns, and reproductive and defence systems. One who reflects on these facts remembers Allah's verse:

How many creatures do not carry their provision with them! Allah provides for them and He will for you. He is the All-Hearing, the All-Knowing. (Surat al-'Ankabut: 60)

What Illnesses Make One Think About

Man is a being who has many weaknesses and who has to make continual effort to deal with his incompleteness. Illnesses expose man's weakness most explicitly. Therefore, when a friend, or we ourselves, become sick, we have to think about the hidden purpose in it. When we think, we see that even the flu, which is considered a simple illness, offers lessons from which we can take warning. When we catch such an illness, we think the following that firstly, the main cause of flu is a virus so tiny as to be

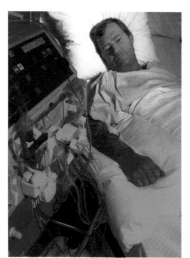

invisible to the naked eye. However, such a tiny organism is enough to cause a man of 60-70 kg to lose his strength, and make him

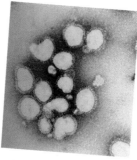

A virus invisible to the naked eye can cause a large human body to be confined to bed.

so exhausted as to prevent him walking or talking. Most of the time, the pills we take or the meals we eat do not do any good. The only thing we can do is rest and wait. In the body, a war takes place in which we cannot intervene. We are tied hand and foot by a tiny organism. In such a situation, what we should first remember is the following verse of Allah, in which prophet Ibrahim says:

> **He Who created me and guides me;**
> **He Who gives me food and gives me drink;**
> **And when I am ill, it is He Who heals me;**
> **He Who will cause my death, then give me life;**
> **He Who I sincerely hope will forgive my mistakes on the Day of Reckoning.**
> **My Lord, give me right judgement and unite me with the righteous. (Surat Ash-Shu'ara': 79-83)**

A person who catches any type of illness should compare his attitude in good health to his attitude during his sickness and think about it. He should realise his modest state in times of illness, how strongly he understood that he is in need of Allah, and, for instance, on his way to an operation, how sincerely and strongly he prayed to Allah.

When we witness someone else's illness, we should immediately give thanks to Allah when we remember our own good health. When a believer sees a man with a crippled leg, he should think about what a major and important favour his own leg is to him. He understands that his being able to walk wherever he wants, as soon as he rises in the morning, and to run when necessary or take care of himself without being in need of anyone else, are each great favours of Allah. As he thinks and makes such comparisons, he grasps better the value of the blessings he has been granted.

What Does One Think upon Meeting an Arrogant, Spoiled, Offensive, Bad-Tempered Person?

During the day, in the office or at school, one comes across many different types of people. These people may not all be good-tempered people who fear Allah. The believer who meets such people, is never influenced by them but keeps on sticking to the behaviour commanded by Allah. He knows that the reason for the bad character traits of these people is their lack of fear of Allah and their disbelief in the hereafter. And the following flows through his mind: Allah warns people about the agony of hell and asks them to think of endless torment and amend their conduct in the life of this world, turn humbly towards Allah and live sincerely by the religion. If one realises that he is face to face with such a serious threat, he will certainly take precautions to avoid it. Yet, those who do not think about it and therefore do not comprehend its seriousness, act as if there is no place of fire and torment being prepared for them.

Someone who is aware of these facts, remembers some other very important matters. While waiting at the edge of the fire of hell, the attitudes of each one of these people will be completely different. If someone, who does not hesitate to display spoiled, impudent and arrogant manners today, lacking all belief in Allah, is arrested on the Day of Reckoning and brought before the pit of hell dragged on the ground and subjected to constant degradation, then the expression on his face, his attitude, the way he speaks or the words he uses will not be as they used to be.

If an aggressive, insolent disbeliever, habitually commits crimes and has no human aspect, is brought to the edge of the fire of hell, he will feel eternal regret when he sees its torment.

Someone who makes all kinds of excuses for not living by the religion and not worshipping Allah in the life of this world, will not be able to make the same excuses waiting in front of the gate of hell. At that time, prostration will no longer be possible even though the disbeliever wants to perform it, and prayer will no longer be answered even though the disbeliever prays earnestly.

Someone who fears Allah never forgets these matters. He thinks about the fire of hell and by virtue of it sees what right manners,

> *Those who took their religion as a diversion and a game, and were deluded by the life of the world. Today We will forget them just as they forgot the encounter of this Day and denied Our Signs. (Surat al-A'raf: 51)*

right words, and good character are. Since he has a strong faith in the existence of hell and constantly thinks about it, he always acts as if he is right next to the hell fire, and always thinks about the fact that he will be called to account for everything he does.

Allah calls people to think of hell and the Day of Reckoning:

On the Day that each self finds the good it did, and the evil it did, present there in front of it, it will wish there were an age between it and then. Allah advises you to beware of Him. Allah is Ever-Gentle with His slaves. (Surat Al 'Imran: 30)

While Eating...

It is Allah Who made the earth a stable home for you and the sky a dome, and formed you, giving you the best of forms, and provided you with good and wholesome things. That is Allah, your Lord. Blessed be Allah, the Lord of all the worlds. (Surah Ghafir: 64)

Allah has given people diverse, pure, delicious food and drink in the world. Certainly, all these are manifestations of Allah's endless grace and His mercy to people. People could well live their lives with only one kind of food and drink but Allah has bestowed upon them countless favours: fruits, vegetables and various kinds of meats...

A believer who knows that all these favours are from Allah, thinks about them and gives thanks to Allah every time he sits down to a meal.

Allah has given people various kinds of food. The presence of thousands of kinds of food with various tastes and fragrances is an indication of Allah's mercy to people.

Of What Do Fruits Served During a Meal Make One Think?

In many verses of the Qur'an, Allah mentions that He blesses people with many kinds of food. These foods are there in front of anyone who sits down to a meal. The dining table is decked with various vegetables

grown from the soil, and many animal products. Man, by nature, is created to find pleasure in these foods. These foods, each one more delicious than the next, are at the same time necessary for our survival. Let us think about what we would do if these nourishing foods, so necessary for our survival, had no taste, or if they tasted bad, or if they were harmful to us despite their pleasant taste, or if there were only a few kinds of food on which we fed, solely for survival. Allah's mercy to us is the only reason we are faced, not with tasteless food and drink but with such a picture as we see on the table. Even if one thinks only of fruit, one will recognise the tremendous favour shown us.

The conscientious person, who sees a large variety of fruit on the dining table, thinks the following:

◆ That out of the dark soil come fruits of diverse colours, a variety of fragrances, with extremely clean contents, each of which has a very pleasant taste, is a great favour Allah grants people.

◆ The banana, tangerine, orange, melon, and watermelon, in short all fruits, are created each with its wrappings. Their peels protect fruits

Allah is He Who created the heavens and the earth and sends down water from the sky and by it brings forth fruits as provision for you... (Surah Ibrahim: 32)

from decay and ruin. Their fragrances are also preserved in these wrappings. Soon after their wrappings are removed, they begin to turn black and spoil.

◆ When examined one by one, the fruits are seen to have many delicate points of significance. The tangerine and orange, for example, are segmented. If they were a single piece, it would have been more difficult to eat such juicy fruits. Yet, Allah has fashioned them in slices for people's convenience. Unquestionably, this flawless, extremely aesthetical design, perfectly addressing our needs, is one of the signs of the creation of Allah, the Most Knowing.

◆ The strawberry, for example, is a very special fruit with its particular form and taste. The patterns on it seem as if they are meticulously designed. With its refreshing red form crowned with green leaves, it is one of the works of the matchless art of Allah. The sweetness in its fragrance and taste, and its being seedless and skinless, make it easy to eat thus reminding one the fruits of Paradise. That a fruit, which almost entirely grows in the soil, has such a beautiful and striking colour, is a very strong sign to us from our Lord Who creates it and Who manifests His art, wisdom and knowledge in the things He creates.

◆ The presence of different fruits in each season is another subject to think about. It is a favour and grace of Allah to people that, for example, in winter, a period when people need vitamins most, such C vitamin-rich fruits as tangerines, oranges and grapefruits are available, while in summer, such fruits as cherries and thirst-quenching melons, watermelons and peaches are abundant.

◆ The charming picture of fruits on their branches or as they are planted is one which Allah presents us. The picture of hundreds of fruits on the apparently bone-dry branch, tightly fastened to it and juicy inside, some of them as if specially polished outside, is evidence that each one of them has been created by Allah. For instance, bunches of grapes look as if they have been placed on the branches of the grapevine one by one. Allah has created each one of them as a unique creation. Their appearance on their branches is fashioned in such a way as to appeal to people. For this reason, while depicting paradise in the Qur'an, Allah states that its fruits are ready to be picked, in the verse, **"Its shading branches will droop down over them, its ripe fruit hanging ready to be picked"** (Surat al-Insan: 14).

Certainly, what are mentioned here are only a few restricted examples. The blessings Allah creates are too diverse to be counted. He who realises this at the dining table remembers another verse of Allah.

Is He Who creates like him who does not create? So will you not pay heed? If you tried to number Allah's blessings, you could never count them. Allah is Ever-Forgiving, Most Merciful. (Surat an-Nahl: 17-18)

What Flavours and Odours Make One Think

Continuing to think, we come to realise more the beauties and subtleties in the creation of Allah. While pondering all these, a conscientious person also thinks that it is a great favour of his Lord that he is able to derive pleasure from the blessings that Allah offers. He remembers that the senses of taste and smell, in particular, help us perceive many of the world's beauties. And he goes on to think that if we did not have the sense of smell, we could not take as much pleasure as we now do from a rose, from the fruits we eat or even from a barbecue. If we did not have the sense of taste, we would not recognise the unique tastes of chocolate, candies, meat, strawberries and other blessings.

We must not forget that we might well have been living in a colourless, tasteless and odourless world. And if Allah had not given us all these as blessings, we could by no means have acquired them. Yet, Allah has bestowed upon people His favour by creating tastes and smells as well as the sensory systems to perceive them.

Every view we enjoy presents us the art of Allah. Upon seeing the beauty of a garden, one should exalt Allah saying, "It is as Allah wills, there is no strength but in Allah."

All beauty one sees in nature is evidence of Allah's exalted and unique power of creation. Paradise, on the other hand, is too flawless to be compared to the beauty of the world.

While Strolling In the Garden...
What Beauties Seen in Nature Make One Think

He who believes in Allah praises his Lord for the beauties he sees in nature. He is aware that Allah has created all existing beauty. He knows that all these beauties belong to Allah and they are manifestations of His attribute of jamal – beauty.

While walking in nature, one encounters more beauty. From a single straw to the yellow daisy, from birds to ants, everything is full of details, which need reflection. As people reflect upon these, they come to understand the power and might of Allah.

Butterflies, for example, are very aesthetically pleasing creatures. With the symmetry and design of their lace-like wings – which are extremely precise as if drawn by hand – their harmonious, phosphorescent colours, butterflies are evidence of Allah's unequalled art and superior power of creation.

Similarly, innumerable plant and tree varieties on earth are among the beauties Allah creates. Flowers, all in different colours and trees of different forms, have been created and among their purposes is that they give great pleasure to people.

One who has faith thinks about how flowers such as the rose, violet, daisy, hyacinth, carnation, orchid and others have such smooth surfaces, and how they come out of their seed completely flat without any puckers as if ironed.

Other wonders Allah creates are the fragrances of these flowers. A rose, for instance, has a strong and constant ever-changing smell. Even with the latest technology, scientists cannot develop an exact match of the smell of the rose. Laboratory research to imitate this smell has not yielded satisfactory results. Smells produced based on the scent of the rose are generally heavy and disturbing. However, the original scent of the rose does not disturb.

Someone who has faith knows that each one of these is created for him to praise Allah, to present him the art and knowledge of Allah in the beauty He creates. For this reason, when someone sees this beauty while strolling in the garden, he glorifies Allah, saying, **"It is as Allah wills, there is no strength but in Allah"** (Surat al-Kahf: 39). He remembers that Allah has put all this beauty at the service of mankind and that He will give the believers incomparably excellent blessings in the hereafter. And because of this, his love for Allah increases ever more.

Flowers developing from their buds without being puckered at all as if ironed.

Have You Ever Thought about an Ant which You Have Seen While Walking in a Garden?

People, in general, do not see any sense in thinking about the living things they see in their surroundings. They do not imagine that those living things they come across every day may have very interesting features. For a person who has faith, on the other hand, every living thing Allah creates bears the traces of a perfect creation. Ants, too, are some of these creatures.

Someone who believes does not turn a blind eye to the ants he sees while wandering in the garden. By seeing their astonishing features, he witnesses the perfect creation of Allah.

Even examining the movement of the ant is thought provoking. It moves its infinitesimal legs in a sequential and extremely organised manner knowing perfectly which leg should take the first step and which the next. It moves very rapidly without faltering.

This tiny insect lifts crumbs much bigger than its body. It carries them to its nest with heart and soul. It travels distances that are very long in comparison to its tiny body. On featureless land, with no guide at its service, it can easily find its nest. Despite the entrance of the nest being too small even for us to find, it is not confused and finds it no matter where it is.

When one sees in the garden those ants, lined up one after the other, ardently toiling to carry food to their nest, one cannot stop wondering what kind of purpose these tiny living beings might have in working so hard. Then one realises that not only does the ant carry food for itself, but also for other members of its colony, for the queen ant and baby ants. How such a tiny ant, which does not even have a developed brain,

An ant industriously carrying food to its nest.

knows diligence, discipline and self-sacrifice is a point on which one needs to reflect. After pondering these facts, one reaches the following conclusion: ants, like all other living beings, act by the inspiration of Allah and obey His commands alone.

What the "Conscious" Movements of Ivy Make One Think

A believer strolling in the garden also thinks about the ivy that he encounters, which is one of the beautiful things that Allah creates. For a man who reflects, there are signs to learn from every living thing.

For instance, the ivy's winding itself round a branch or any other object is an event about which one needs to think carefully. If the development of the ivy were recorded, and then the replay speeded up, it would be seen that the ivy moves as if it is a conscious being. Just as if it sees that there is a branch right before it, it extends itself toward that branch and it fastens itself to the branch as though lassooing it. Sometimes it winds around the branch several times to secure itself. It grows very rapidly in this fashion and it makes itself a new way, either returning or proceeding downwards, when its path comes to an end. A believer who

The ivy's winding itself around an object looks like the movement of a conscious being.

witnesses all these once again sees that Allah has created all living beings with unique, flawless systems.

As one continues observing the movements of the ivy, one witnesses another important feature of the plant. One sees that the ivy attaches itself firmly to the surface on which it lies by stretching out arms to the sides. The viscous substance this 'unconscious' plant produces is so strong that when one tries to remove it, it may even strip paint off the wall.

The existence of such a plant reveals to the believer, who sees and reflects upon these, the omnipotence of Allah, the Creator of this plant.

What Trees Make One Think

We see trees everyday and everywhere; however, have you ever thought how water reaches the farthest leaf on the top branch of a lofty tree? We can have a better understanding of the extraordinary nature of this by way of a comparison. It is impossible for the water in a tank in the basement of your building to climb to higher floors without a hydrophoric tank or some other powerful engine. You cannot pump water even to the first floor. Therefore, there should also be in trees a pumping system similar to the hydrophoric engine. Otherwise, since water would not be able to reach the trunk of the tree and the branches, trees would soon die.

Allah has created each tree with all the necessary equipment. Moreover, the hydraulic system in many trees is too superior to be compared to the building in which one lives. That is one of the subjects someone, who looks at everything with "an eye which actually sees", thinks upon seeing these plants.

Another subject has to do with the leaves. Someone who reflects on the things he sees does not, upon looking at a tree, consider the leaves as common forms, which he is accustomed to see. He thinks of various things that do not occur to most people. Leaves, for example, are very delicate forms. Nonetheless, they do not dry out under the scorching heat. When a human stays out in a temperature of 40°C even for a short while, the colour of his skin changes and he suffers from dehydration. Leaves, on the other hand, can remain green under the burning heat, without being scorched,

Bright green and living leaves growing out of the dry wood of a branch, water reaching the threadlike veins of the leaves at heights of many metres, the leaves not drying out under the burning sun... these are only a few of the numerous subjects about which trees make one think.

for days, and even months, although very little amounts of water drain through their threadlike veins. That is a miracle of creation demonstrating that Allah creates everything with an unequalled knowledge. Thinking over this miracle of creation, someone who believes can once again see the might of Allah and remember Him.

While Reading a Paper or Watching TV...

People follow the daily papers and TV news either during the day or when they return home in the evening. In such reports, there are many issues for a conscientious person to think over, take heed from, and in which to see the signs of Allah.

What the Frequency of Cases of Violence, Robbery and Homicide Make One Think

Everyday, on the local pages of the newspapers or on TV news, one comes across many reports of homicide, wounding, theft, robbery, swindle and suicide. The frequent occurrence of these events, and a large number of people's being so disposed to commit such crimes indicate the harm from which people who do not live by the religion of Allah suffer. Someone's kidnapping a small child for ransom, causing him great fear,

In societies that fear Allah, none of these scenes take place

and even killing him, another's pointing a gun at the face of a man and shooting him without hesitation, another's accepting a bribe, or committing suicide or swindling... all these are indications that these people do not fear Allah and do not believe in the hereafter. Someone who fears Allah and knows that he will give account in the hereafter would never do any of these. Each of these are acts that will be recompensed with hell in the hereafter, if the perpetrator does not turn in repentance from them and if Allah does not forgive and show mercy.

Someone may say: "I am an atheist. I do not believe in Allah, yet I do not accept bribes". However, this statement of a man with no fear of Allah is not at all convincing. It is very likely that he would decline to keep this promise if the conditions change. For instance, if this person has to find money for a very urgent cause, and happens to be in a situation in which he has the chance to steal or accept a bribe, he might not hold his promise. Or such a person is not expected to keep his word when his own life is at stake. Although this person may avoid taking bribes in difficult situations, he may be apt to commit other forbidden acts. A person who believes, however, never does anything whatsoever for which he cannot give account in the hereafter.

So, the cause of the events that make us voice protests in the newspapers, on TV, in our social lives, and urge us to exclaim "what happened to this society?" is, in truth, lack of religion. A believer who sees these reports does not turn a blind eye to them but thinks that the only solution is to tell people about the religion and to revive the values of the religion. In a society made up of people who fear Allah and who know that they will give account in the hereafter, it is impossible for these kinds of events to occur to the extent they do now in our time. In such a society, peace and safety will be lived at the highest level.

What Discussion Programmes Lasting till Morning Make One Think

For a person who continues to think over the things he sees around him, discussion programmes broadcast on TV are also examples for him to think about.

These discussion programmes include people who are most closely involved with the topic of the day and who are most knowledgeable about that subject. These people discuss a topic for hours, with no one being able to work out a solution or reach a conclusion. However, those who attend these discussion programmes are people who are considered to be qualified to solve these issues.

Indeed, the solution to most of these issues is quite clear. However, people's self-interests, their remaining under the influence of their immediate circle, their efforts to push themselves forward rather than sincerely seeking for solutions, bring them to deadlock and stalemate.

A conscientious person who witnesses all these, thinks that the reason for these events, too, lies in society's being distant from the religion of Allah. Someone who believes in Allah never displays an irresponsible, barren, and heedless attitude. He knows that there is good in every event to which Allah exposes him, that he is constantly being tested in this world, that he has to use his reason, strength and knowledge in such a way as to please Allah.

In addition, while watching such programme, the believer remembers a verse of Allah:

... more than anything else, man is argumentative (Surat al-Kahf: 54)

The atmosphere in these kinds of programmes discloses the argumentative and disputatious nature of people. These people's failure most of the time even to understand the question, their being obsessed only with what they will say and trying to say it first, their interrupting one another, their easily raising their voices and losing their tempers in a flash, and their starting to hurl insults at each other, clearly reveal the negative aspects of apparently educated and sophisticated people who lack the religion of Allah.

In the company of one hundred percent sincere and honest people who fear Allah, such prolonged and fruitless scenes never take place. As the purpose is to find the solution that most pleases Allah and is of maximum use to people, the most proper and conscientious method of rea-soning is found and put into practice without losing any time. Since every-body's conscience will be contented with the final decision, no dispute takes place.

If anyone has an objection grounded on reasonable causes that shows a better way, then his suggestion is employed right away. Unlike others, those who fear Allah do not display an obstinate and arrogant attitude. Remembering what Allah says in the Qur'an; "**... Over everyone with knowledge there is one more knowing**" (Surah Yusuf: 76), they employ the best options that they can.

These discussions, lasting until the morning without reaching any solution, are worth considering because they show what can happen in an environment where the values and high qualities of character of religion are not lived.

What Famine and Poverty in Every Corner of the World Make One Think

One of the issues frequently dealt with in the media is injustice among people.

While there are, on one side of the world, notably prosperous coun-tries with very high levels of welfare, there are, on the other side, people who do not have anything to eat, medicines to treat even the simplest dis-eases, and who repeatedly die of neglect. The first thing that this situation reveals is the iniquitous system prevailing in the world. It would be very easy for one or more of the wealthy countries to save those people. For instance, near the nations dying of hunger in Africa, there are communi-ties who have accumulated wealth from diamond mines and hence devel-oped an advanced 'civilisation'. Although it is quite easy to relocate those people who live in poverty, near to starvation and are abandoned to die, or to provide means to meet their needs in the areas where they live, for decades no fundamental solution has been sought for these people. However, helping these people is not a task that a few people can handle. In order to find fundamental solutions, many people need to make self-sacrifices. However, today, the number of people who lay claim to attempting to solve such a problem is quite few.

Trillions of dollars are being wasted in every part of the world for various reasons. On the one hand, that some people throw their meals away unsatisfied with the amount of salt, and, on the other hand, that some die unable to find enough food to eat, is clear evidence against an iniquitous world order caused by not living by the values of the religion on the earth.

Someone who sees all these thinks that the only thing that will eliminate this iniquity is the adoption of the values that Allah commands. People who fear Allah and act by their consciences would never allow such iniquity and injustice. They would help out needy people with quick, definite and long-lasting solutions not allowing any ostentation, and, if necessary, exploiting all the possibilities of the world.

Allah tells us in the Qur'an that helping the poor and needy is a characteristic of people who fear Allah and the Day of Judgement:

Those in whose wealth there is a known share for beggars and the destitute; those who affirm the Day of Judgement, those who are fearful of the punishment of their Lord. (Surat al-Ma'arij: 24-27)

They give food, despite their love for it, to the poor and orphans and captives: 'We feed you only out of desire for the Face of Allah. We do not want any repayment from you or any thanks. Truly we fear from our Lord a glowering, calamitous Day.' (Surat al-Insan: 8-10)

Do they not see that they are tried once or twice in every year? But still they do not turn back. They do not pay heed. (Surat at-Tawba: 126)

Not feeding the poor is a characteristic of irreligious people who have no fear of Allah:

(Allah commands) 'Seize him and truss him up. Then roast him in the Blazing Fire. Then bind him in a chain which is

seventy cubits long. He used not to believe in Allah the Most Great, nor did he urge the feeding of the poor. Therefore here today he has no friend nor any food except exuding pus which no one will eat except those who were in error.' (Surat al-Haqqa: 30-37)

What Disasters Occurring Around the World Make One Think

Some of the reports people frequently run across on TVs and in newspapers are of disasters. People may meet disaster at any time. A powerful earthquake may happen, a fire may start or flooding may occur. Someone who sees these reports remembers that Allah has power over all things, that He can raze a city to the ground if He so wills. Thinking of these, one sees that there is no one but Allah with whom one can take refuge and from whom one can ask help. Even the strongest buildings and cities equipped with the most advanced technology cannot stand against the power of Allah; they too can perish all of a sudden.

There are hidden meanings to be reflected on in the disaster reports frequently covered by newspapers and TV.

1. A flood disaster in Honduras. 2. A disaster in Mali-Gao caused by gusty winds. 3. A town of the coast inundated by river floods. 4. Another inundated town. 5. A devastated town.

All these scenes are for men to think about and take lessons from.

Someone who hears about or reads these disaster reports also reflects that Allah has sent a disaster against this city for a purpose. In the Qur'an, Allah relates that He consigns the disobedient nations to penalty so that they might take heed or be repaid for their deeds. Hence, if a given community practises values with which Allah would be displeased, Allah may have punished them for that reason. Or, it may be that Allah is testing these people with some hardships in the world.

Thinking about these possibilities, the believer fears that all these may also befall him, and asks forgiveness of Allah for his own conduct.

No person and no nation can prevent any disaster from occurring

unless Allah so wills. It makes no difference whether it is the most wealthy and powerful country in the world or a place that ordinarily would be thought to be at little risk because of its geographical location. Allah says that no nation can prevent a disaster that will befall them.

> **Do the people of the cities feel secure against Our violent force coming down on them in the night while they are asleep? Or do the people of the cities feel secure against Our violent force coming down on them in the day while they are playing games? Do they feel secure against Allah's devising? No one feels secure against Allah's devising except for those who are lost. Is it not clear to those who have inherited the earth after these people**

An earthquake lasting a few seconds is enough to destroy a whole city. Those who think that these scenes are 'works of nature' are mistaken. This is because nature, an incredibly ill-defined entity, just as all other beings, under the command of Allah.

that, if We wanted to, We could strike them for their wrong actions, sealing up their hearts so that they cannot hear? (Surat al-A'raf: 97-100)

What News Items About Usury Make One Think

Another topic frequently dealt with in the news is decline in the economy. In particular, a number of negative news items are reported about usury each day. Someone who reads the reports mentioning that usury is out of control, and causes downturns in the economy realises that in return for the wide adoption of such a deeply abhorrent and forbidden act, Allah depresses the productivity of people's earnings. As stated in the verse, **"Allah obliterates usury but makes charitable deeds grow in value! Allah does not love any persistently ungrateful wrongdoer"** (Surat al-Baqara: 276), Allah eliminates the profit earned through usury, and decrease its productivity. This fact is stated in another verse as follows:

You who believe! do not feed on usury, multiplied and then remultiplied. Have taqwa of Allah so that hopefully you will be successful. (Surat Al 'Imran: 130)

What you give with usurious intent, aiming to get back a greater amount from people's wealth, does not become greater with Allah. But anything you give as charity, seeking the Face of Allah, all who do that will get a recompense multiplied. (Surat ar-Rum: 39)

For a man who reflects, reports about usury, too, are examples that Allah's verses are manifest among people.

Thinking about Nice Places

It is also possible to see on TV programs, in newspapers and magazines the beauty Allah creates and to reflect on it. Looking at or visiting somewhere with a wonderful view, a beautiful house, garden or beach surely pleases everyone. These views, first of all, remind one of paradise. A believing person remembers once more that Allah, Who gives such great blessings, and shows people such glorious beauty, will certainly create incomparable places in paradise.

Someone who sees these also thinks the following: every beauty created in the world has a number of flaws and imperfections because the world is a place of testing. Someone who spends some time at a holiday resort, the images of which he has earlier seen on TV, notices these defects. The weather's extreme humidity, the sea's disturbing saline content, the blistering heat and flies; these are only a few examples. Many worldly difficulties can happen, such as sunburn, the travel agency's organisational problems, and the intolerable nature of the people with whom one shares the place.

In paradise, there will be the originals of these beauties and there will not be a single thing that would disturb one, and not a single displeasing conversation will be held. In every beauty a believer confronts in the world, he longs for paradise. He always gives thanks for the blessings Allah has given him in the world, and he takes pleasure from them thinking that all these are blessings Allah has given him out of His grace. Knowing, however, that the originals of these beautiful things exist in paradise, he does not forget the hereafter by being carried away by the beauty of the world. He leads a life by means of which he can come to possess eternal beauty and deserve to enter the paradise of Allah.

What Does It Make One Think on Reading in Scientific Magazines that The Building Block of Matter is the Atom?

Unless man thinks over the things he knows, he cannot grasp the subtleties in them and realise in what an extraordinary environment he lives. On that account, a person who believes continually thinks over the living beings and events Allah creates. These can sometimes be subjects known to many people, yet he is able to draw different conclusions from them than others do.

For example, it is a very well known fact that the basic component of every animate or inanimate being in the universe is the atom. That is, most people know that the books they read, the armchairs on which they sit, the water they drink and all the things they see around them are composed of atoms. Yet only conscientious people think beyond this and witness the exalted might of Allah.

When such people see reports about this subject, they think the following: atoms are inanimate beings. How, then, can inanimate substances such as atoms come together and form animate human beings capable of seeing, hearing, interpreting what they hear, enjoying the music to which they listen, thinking, making decisions, being happy or miserable? How

Have you ever thought that the building blocks of your watch, the food you eat, the building in which you live, your car, your glasses, your pet, the flowers in your garden, your computer, the seas, the sky and your body are the same ATOMS?

could man acquire such traits making him totally different from other conglomerates of atoms?

Certainly, inanimate and unconscious atoms cannot give human beings these human qualities. It is clear that Allah creates man with a spirit endowed with such characteristics. This reminds one of a verse of Allah:

He Who has created all things in the best possible way. He commenced the creation of man from clay; then produced his seed from an extract of base fluid; then formed him and breathed His Spirit into him and gave you hearing, sight, and hearts. What little thanks you show! (Surat as-Sajda: 7-9)

Some Facts One Reaches by Deep Thinking

Have you ever thought that everything is created for man only?

When someone who believes in Allah investigates the systems and all the animate and inanimate beings present in the universe with an attentive eye, he sees that all are created for man. He understands that nothing has come into existence by chance but Allah creates everything in the most precise way for man's use.

Man, for example, can breathe effortlessly all the time. The air he

The planet and the whole universe in which we live bear all the properties necessary for our lives. Someone who thinks about this will see clearly that Allah created the whole universe for us.

inhales neither burns his nasal passages nor makes him dizzy nor causes headaches. The proportion of the gases in air is designed with the amounts that are most suitable for the human body. Someone who thinks of these remembers another very crucial point: if the oxygen concentration in the atmosphere were a little more or a little less than at present, in both cases life would vanish. He then remembers what a hard time he has in breathing in airless places. As a believing person continues to think on this subject, he constantly gives thanks to his Lord. This is because he sees that the atmosphere of the earth could well be designed, as it is on many other planets, so as to make it difficult to breathe. Yet, it is not so and the atmosphere of the earth is created in perfect balance and order in such a way as to enable billions of people to breathe effortlessly.

Someone who keeps thinking about the planet on which he lives, thinks how important water, which Allah creates, is for human life. The following comes to mind: people, in general, understand the importance of water only when they are deprived of it for a long time. Water, however, is a substance which we need every moment of our lives. For instance, a considerable portion of our body cells and of the blood that reaches every point in our body consists of water. Were it not so, the fluidity of blood would decrease and its flow in the veins would become very difficult. The fluidity of water is important not only for our bodies but also for plants. Thus, water reaches the furthest end of the leaf by passing through its thread-like vessels.

The great quantity of water in the seas makes our earth habitable. If the proportion of sea to land on the earth were smaller, then lands would turn into deserts and life would be impossible.

A conscientious person who thinks about these matters is completely convinced that the establishment of such a perfect balance on the earth is surely not a coincidence. Seeing and thinking about all these shows that a Creator Who is exalted and the owner of eternal power created everything for a purpose.

Moreover, he also remembers that the examples on which he has been reflecting are very limited in number. Indeed, it is impossible to count the examples regarding the delicate balances on earth. Yet a man who reflects can readily see the order, perfection and balance that prevail in every corner of the universe, and thus reach the conclusion that Allah has created everything for man. Allah states this in the Qur'an thus:

And He has made everything in the heavens and everything on the earth subservient to you. It is all from Him. There are certainly Signs in that for people who reflect. (Surat al-Jathiyya: 13)

What Eternity Makes One Think

Everyone is familiar with the concept of eternity, yet have you every thought about eternity? This is one of the subjects upon which a person believing in Allah reflects.

Allah's creating the eternal life of paradise and hell is a very important subject over which everyone needs to think. One who thinks it over poses the following questions: the eternal nature of paradise is one of the greatest blessings and rewards bestowed in the life after death. The glorious life in paradise will never end. Man may live in this world for at most a hundred year. Life in paradise, however, is timeless, so that in comparison a quadrillion times quadrillion years is short.

Someone who remembers these also realises that it is quite difficult for man to comprehend eternity. Such an example may help elucidate this subject: if there were a quadrillion people who had kept going a quadrillion times a quadrillion, night and day, and if each of them had a life of a quadrillion years all of which they spent for this end, the figure they would reach in total would still remain like "zero" in comparison to the number of years to be spent in the eternal life.

Someone who thinks on these reaches the following conclusion: Allah possesses such great knowledge that what is "everlasting" for man, in His sight has already ended. Every incident and every thought that have taken place from the first moment time began to its last moment are, with their times and forms, determined and come to an end within His knowledge.

One should, in the same way, think that hell is a place in which unbelievers will dwell forever. There are various kinds of torture, torments, and distresses in hell. Unbelievers in hell are subject to uninterrupted physical and spiritual torture, which never stops, nor is the sufferer spared any time for sleep or rest. If there were an end to the life in hell, there would be hope for the companions of hell even if that rest were quadrillions of years later. Yet, what they receive in return for their associating partners with Allah and their disbelief is eternal torment.

As for those who reject Our Signs and are arrogant regarding them, they are the Companions of the Fire, remaining in it timelessly, for ever. (Surat al-A'raf: 36)

It is extremely important for each individual to try to comprehend eternity by reflecting on it. It increases man's endeavours for the hereafter, and reinforces both his fear and his hope. While he strongly fears eternal torment, he cherishes the hope of attaining eternal bliss.

What Does One Think About Dreams?

There are important purposes in dreams for someone who reflects. Such a person thinks about how "realistic" the dreams are that he sees while asleep, which in that way are no different in their realism from the moment he awakes. For instance, despite one person's body lying on the bed, in dream he went on business trips, met new people, and had lunch while listening to music. He enjoyed the taste of his meal, danced to the music, became excited because of the incidents that happened, became happy and unhappy, was afraid and felt tired. He could even have driven a vehicle that he had not previously driven until that day and did not even know how to drive.

Although his body had been lying still in bed, his eyes shut, he saw different images from those of the place where he was. This means that what saw was not the eyes. Although the room in which he was lying was empty, he heard voices. Thus what heard was not the ears. Everything had taken place in his brain. Still, everything was very realistic as if every image had an original form. What is it, then, that although none of them has originals in the external world, forms such realistic images in the brain? Man cannot formulate these consciously and intentionally while asleep. Nor can the brain produce such images on its own. The brain is a bulk of meat made up of protein molecules. It would be extremely unreasonable to claim that such a substance forms images on its own, and that it even forms human faces, places and sounds

Allah takes back people's selves when their death arrives and those who have not yet died, while they are asleep. He keeps hold of those whose death has been decreed and sends the others back for a specified term. There are certainly Signs in that for people who reflect.
(Surat az-Zumar: 42)

never seen or heard before that day. Who is it, then, that shows the images in the dream while asleep? One who reflects upon such questions once again sees the obvious truth: it is Allah Who makes men sleep, takes back their souls while they are asleep, sends them back to them when they awake and shows them their dreams in sleep.

Someone who knows that Allah shows the dreams also reflects upon the dream's hidden purposes and the reasons for their creation. In one's dream, one is as sure of the people and events he experiences as when awake. We think that all of them really exist, that the lives we dream are uninterrupted and continuous. If somebody comes up to us and says, "You are having a dream now, wake up", we would not believe him. Someone who realises this, on the other hand, thinks as follows: "Who can say that the life of this world is not also a temporary and dream-like life? Just as I wake up from a dream, one day I will also wake up from the life of this world and see totally different images, for instance, the images of the here-after..."

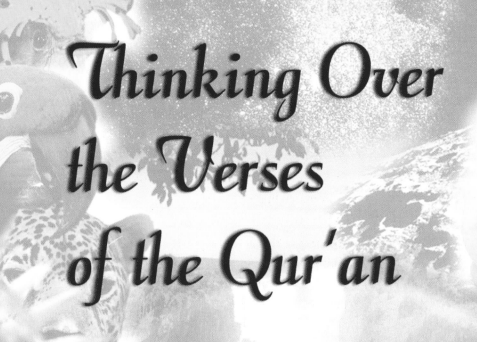

Thinking Over
the Verses
of the Qur'an

*T*he Qur'an is the last book Allah sent to all people. Every person living on the earth is responsible for learning the Qur'an and fulfilling the commands communicated in it. Most people, however, do not learn it and fulfil what Allah commands in the Qur'an, although they accept it as a divine book. This is a consequence of their not thinking about the Qur'an, but knowing it by information gained here and there. For a man who reflects, on the other hand, the importance of the Qur'an and its place in man's life is very great.

First of all, someone who "reflects" wants to know his Creator Who created him and the universe in which he lives, gave him life when he was nothing, and bestowed countless blessings and beautiful things on him. Someone like that wants to learn what kind of conduct He would be pleased with. The Qur'an, which Allah sent through His Messenger, is a guide answering the questions above. For this reason, man needs to know the book Allah revealed to people as a guide and in which He distinguished good from evil. He needs to ponder over each verse and fulfil what Allah orders in the most proper and pleasing way.

Allah states the purpose for which the Qur'an was revealed to people:

> **It (the Qur'an) is a Book We have sent down to you, full of blessing, so let people of intelligence ponder its Signs and take heed. (Surah Sad: 29)**
>
> **No indeed! It (the Qur'an) is a reminder to which anyone who wills may pay heed. But they will only heed if Allah wills. He is entitled to be feared and entitled to forgive. (Surat al-Muddaththir: 54-55)**

Many people read the Qur'an, but the important thing is, just as Allah states in His verses, to ponder on each verse of the Qur'an, to draw a lesson from that verse and improve one's conducts in compliance with these lessons. Someone who reads the verse, **"For truly with hardship comes ease; truly with hardship comes ease,"** (Surat al-Inshirah: 5-6), for example, reflects upon it. He understands that Allah creates ease with each hardship, and therefore, the only thing he has to do when he meets hardship is to put his trust in Allah and find the ease that is with it. Allah's promise being so, we see that giving up hope or being stricken with panic in moments of difficulty is a sign of a weakness in our faith. After reading this verse and reflecting upon it, our conduct will agree with the verse throughout our lives.

In the Qur'an, Allah relates stories from the lives of the prophets and messengers who lived in the past, so that people can see how are the conduct, conversation and lives of a person with whom Allah is pleased, and take them as examples. Allah states in some of His verses that people must think over the stories of the messengers and draw lessons from them:

There is an instruction in their stories for people of intelligence. (Surah Yusuf: 111)

And (We left a Sign) also in Musa when We sent him to Pharaoh with clear authority. (Surat adh-Dhariyat: 38)

We rescued him (Nuh) and the occupants of the Ark and made that into a Sign for all the worlds. (Surat al-'Ankabut: 15)

In the Qur'an, some of the attributes of past nations, their manners and the disasters that befell them are mentioned. It would be a great misconception to read these verses merely as the narration of historical events in which is related that which has befallen past nations. This is because, just as in all other verses, Allah has revealed the verses about past nations for us to think over, and for us to amend our conduct by deriving lessons from the events that befell these nations:

We destroyed those of your kind in the past. But is there any rememberer there? (Surat al-Qamar: 51)

We bore him on a planked and well-caulked ship, which ran before Our eyes – a reward for him who had been rejected. We left it as a Sign. But is there any rememberer there? How terrible were My punishment and warnings! We have made the Qur'an easy to remember. But is there any rememberer there? (Surat al-Qamar: 13-17)

Allah has revealed the Qur'an as a guide to all people. Therefore, reflecting upon every verse of the Qur'an, and living according to it by deriving lessons and warnings from every verse is the only way to gain the approval, mercy and the paradise of Allah.

What does Allah Summon People to Think about in the Qur'an?

And We have sent down the Reminder to you so that you can make clear to mankind what has been sent down to them so that hopefully they will reflect. (Surat an-Nahl: 44)

Just as in this ayah of Surat an-Nahl, in many other of His ayat, Allah summons people to reflect. Thinking over the things Allah calls us to think about and seeing the hidden purposes and the creational miracles our Lord has created is an act of worship. Each subject on which we reflect helps us to further understand and appreciate the omnipotence, wisdom, knowledge, art and other attributes of Allah.

Allah Summons Man to Think over His Own Creation

Man says, "When I am dead, will I then be brought out again alive?" **Does not man recall** that We created him before when he was not anything? (Surah Maryam: 66-67)

Allah Summons People to Think Over the Creation of the Universe

In the creation of the heavens and earth, and the alternation of the night and day, and the ships which sail the seas to people's benefit, and the water which Allah sends down from the sky – by which He brings the earth to life when it was dead and scat-

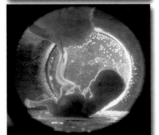

There are many lessons in the creation of man for those who reflect.

ters about in it creatures of every kind – and the varying direction of the winds, and the clouds subservient between heaven and earth, there are Signs **for people who use their intellect**. (Surat al-Baqara: 164)

Allah Summons People to Think over the Temporary Nature of the Life of this World

The metaphor of the life of this world is that of water which We send down from the sky, and which then mingles with the plants of the earth to provide food for both people and animals. Then, when the earth is at its loveliest and takes on its fairest guise and its people think they have it under their control, Our command comes upon it by night or day and We reduce it to dried-out stubble, as though it had not been flourishing just the day before! In this way We make Our Signs clear **for people who reflect**. (Surah Jonah: 24)

Would any of you like to have a garden of dates and grapes, with rivers flowing underneath and containing all kinds of fruits, then to be stricken with old age and have children who are weak, and then for a fierce whirlwind containing fire to come and strike it so that it goes up in flames? In this way Allah makes His Signs clear to you, so that hopefully you reflect. (Surat al-Baqara: 266)

Allah Summons People to Think over the Blessings They Possess

It is He Who stretched out the earth and placed firmly embedded

Man should ponder every animate or inanimate being Allah created.

mountains and rivers in it and made two types of every kind of fruit. He covers over day with night. There are Signs in that **for people who reflect**.

In the earth there are diverse regions side by side and gardens of grapes and cultivated fields, and palm-trees sharing one root and others with individual roots, all watered with the same water. And We make some things better to eat than others. There are Signs in that **for people who use their intellect**. (Surat ar-Ra'd: 3-4)

Allah Summons Man to Think on the Fact that the Whole Universe Has Been Created for Man

And He has made everything in the heavens and everything on the earth subservient to you. It is all from Him. There are certainly Signs in that **for people who reflect**. (Surat al-Jathiya: 13)

And by it He makes crops grow for you and olives and dates and grapes and fruit of every kind. There is certainly a Sign in that **for people who reflect**. He has made night and day subservient to you, and the sun and moon and stars, all subject to His command. There are certainly Signs in that **for people who use their intellect**. And

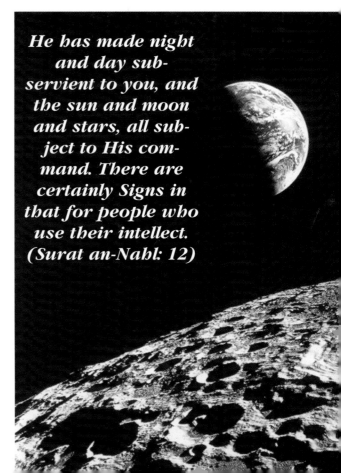

He has made night and day subservient to you, and the sun and moon and stars, all subject to His command. There are certainly Signs in that for people who use their intellect. (Surat an-Nahl: 12)

Attributing the formation of day and night, the movements and the location of the Earth and the Sun to coincidence is great heedlessness. Allah has created day and night only for men.

Have they not looked at the sky above them:
how We structured it and made it beautiful and
how there are no fissures in it? And the earth:
how We stretched it out and cast firmly embed-
ded mountains onto it and caused luxuriant
plants of every kind to grow in it, an instruction
and a reminder for every penitent human being.
(Surah Qaf: 6-8)

also the things of varying colours He has created for you in the earth. There is certainly a Sign in that for people who pay heed. It is He who made the sea subservient to you so that you can eat fresh flesh from it and bring out from it ornaments to wear. And you see the ships cleaving through it so that you can seek His bounty, and so that hopefully you will show thanks. He cast firmly embedded mountains on the earth so it would not move under you, and rivers and pathways so that hopefully you would be guided, and landmarks. And they are guided by the stars. Is He who creates like him who does not create? **So will you not pay heed?** (Surat an-Nahl: 11-17)

Allah Summons People to Think about Their Own Selves

Have they not reflected within themselves? (Surat ar-Rum: 8)

Allah Summons People to Think about Good Values and Deeds

And that you do not go near the property of orphans before they reach maturity – except in a good way; that you give full measure and full weight with justice – We impose on no self any more than it can bear; that you are equitable when you speak – and that you fulfil Allah's contract. That is what He instructs you to do, so that **hopefully you will pay heed**. (Surat al-An'am: 152)

Allah commands justice and doing good and giving to relatives. And He forbids indecency and doing wrong and tyranny. He warns you so that **hopefully you will pay heed**. (Surat an-Nahl: 90)

You who believe! Do not enter houses other than your own until you have asked permission and greeted their inhabitants. That is better for you, so that **hopefully you will pay heed**. (Surat an-Nur: 27)

Allah Summons People to Think about the Hereafter, the Hour, and the Day of Judgement

On the day that each self finds the good it did, and the evil it did, present there in front of it, it will wish there were an age between it and then. Allah advises you to beware of Him. Allah is Ever-Gentle to

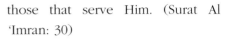

He is Allah. There is no god but Him. Praise be to Him at the first and at the last. Judgement belongs to Him. You will be returned to Him. (Surat al-Qasas: 70)

those that serve Him. (Surat Al 'Imran: 30)

And remember Our servants Ibrahim, Ishaq and Ya'qub, men of true strength and inner sight. We purified their sincerity through **sincere remembrance** of the Abode. (Surah Sad: 45-46)

What are they awaiting but for the Hour to come upon them suddenly? Its Signs have already come. What good will their reminder be to them when it does arrive? (Surah Muhammad: 18)

Allah Summons Man to Think about the Animate Beings He Creates

Your Lord revealed to the bees: "Build dwellings in the mountains and the trees, and also in the structures which men erect. Then eat from every kind of fruit and travel the paths of your Lord, which have

He who reflects can see many extraordinary features in the animate beings Allah creates. This way, he can come to know the endless power and knowledge of Allah.

been made easy for you to follow." From inside them comes a drink of varying colours, containing healing for mankind. There is certainly a Sign in that **for people who reflect**. (Surat an-Nahl: 68-69)

Allah Summons Man to Think about the Punishments That Might Suddenly Befall Him

Say: "**What do you think?** If Allah's punishment were to come upon you or the Hour, would you call on other than Allah if you are being truthful?" (Surat al-An'am: 40)

Say: "**What do you think?** If Allah took away your hearing and your sight and sealed up your hearts, what god is there, other than Allah, who could give them back to you?" Look how We vary the Signs, yet still they turn away! (Surat al-An'am: 46)

Say: "**What do you think?** If Allah's punishment were to come upon you suddenly by night or openly by day, would any but the wrong-doing people be destroyed?" (Surat al-An'am: 47)

Say: "**What do you think?** If His punishment came upon you by night or day, what part of it would the evildoers then try to hasten?" (Surah Yunus: 50)

Do they not see that they are tried once or twice in every year? But still they do not turn back. **They do not pay heed**. (Surat at-Tawba: 126)

We gave Musa the Book after destroying the earlier nations, to awaken people's hearts and as a guidance and a mercy so that **hopefully they would pay heed**. (Surat al-Qasas: 43)

We destroyed those of your kind in the past. But **is there any rememberer there?** (Surat al-Qamar: 51)

We seized Pharaoh's people with years of drought and scarcity of fruits so that **hopefully they would pay heed**. (Surat al-A'raf: 130)

Allah Summons Man to Think about the Qur'an

Will they not ponder the Qur'an? If it had been from other than Allah, they would have found many inconsistencies in it. (Surat an-Nisa': 82)

Do they not ponder the word (of Allah)? Has anything come to them that did not come to their ancestors the previous peoples? (Surat al-Muminun: 68)

It (the Qur'an) is a Book We have sent down to you, full of blessing, so let **people of intelligence ponder its Sign** and take heed. (Surah Sad: 29)

We have made it (the Qur'an) easy in your own tongue so that **hopefully they will pay heed**. (Surat ad-Dukhan: 58)

No indeed! It is truly a reminder to which **anyone who wills may pay heed**. (Surat al-Muddaththir: 54-55)

In this way We have sent it down as an Arabic Qur'an and We have made various threats in it so that hopefully they will have taqwa or **it will spur them into remembrance**. (Surah Ta Ha: 113)

The Messengers of Allah Summoned Their People, Who Lacked Understanding, To Reflect

Say: "I do not say to you that I possess the treasuries of Allah, nor do I know the Unseen, nor do I say to you that I am an angel. I only follow what has been revealed to me." Say: "Are the blind the same as those who can see? So **will you not reflect?**" (Surat al-An'am: 50)

His people argued with him. He said; "Are you arguing with me about Allah when He has guided me? I have no fear of any partner you ascribe to Him unless my Lord should will such a thing to happen. My Lord encompasses all things in His knowledge so **will you not pay heed?** (Surat al-An'am: 80)

Allah Summons People to Resist the Influence of Satan

If an evil impulse from Satan provokes you, seek refuge in Allah. He is All-Hearing, All-Seeing. As for those who have taqwa, when they are bothered by visitors from Satan, **they remember** and immediately see clearly. But as for their brothers, the visitors lead them further into error. And they do not stop at that! (Surat al-A'raf: 200-202)

Allah Encourages the Person to Whom the Message of the Qur'an is Communicated to Think Deeply

Go, you and your brother, with My Signs and do not slacken in remembering Me. Go to Pharaoh; he has overstepped the bounds. But speak to him with gentle words so that **hopefully he will pay heed** or show some fear. (Surah Ta Ha: 42-44)

Allah Invites People to Think about Death and Dreams

Allah takes back people's selves when their death arrives and those who have not yet died, while they are asleep. He keeps hold of those whose death has been decreed and sends the others back for a specified term. There are certainly Signs in that **for people who reflect**. (Surat az-Zumar: 42)

Conclusion

*T*he purpose of this book is a "summons to think". The truth can be told to a person in many different ways; it can be shown by the use of details, pieces of evidence and by every means. Yet, if this person does not think over this truth on his own, sincerely and honestly with the purpose of comprehending the truth, all these efforts are useless. For this reason, when the messengers of Allah communicated the message to their people, they told them the truth clearly and then summoned them to think.

A man who reflects grasps the secrets of Allah's creation, the truth of the life of this world, the existence of hell and paradise, and the inner truth of matters. He gets a deeper understanding of the importance of being a person with whom Allah is pleased, and so he lives religion as is its due, recognises Allah's attributes in everything he sees, and begins to think not according to what the majority of people demand but as Allah commands. As a result, he takes pleasure from beauty much more than others do, and does not suffer distress from baseless misapprehensions and worldly greed.

These are only a few of the beautiful things a person who thinks will gain in the world. The gain in the hereafter of someone who always finds the truth by thinking, is the love, approval, mercy and the paradise of our Lord.

On the other hand, a day is at hand when those who today avoid seeing the truth by thinking will come to think, and moreover, "think deeply and meditate" and see the truth bright clear. Yet their thinking on that day will not be of any use to them but will make them suffer grief. Allah says in the Qur'an when these people will reflect:

When the Great Calamity comes: that Day man will remember what he has striven for and the Blazing Fire will be displayed for all who can see. (Surat an-Nazi'at: 34-36)

Summoning people, who suppose that they can escape from their responsibilities by not thinking, to think so that they may reflect upon the end that will befall them and return to Allah's religion is an act of worship for believers. Yet, as our Lord states in the Qur'an:

... Anyone who will may pay heed. (Surat al-Muddaththir: 55)

Children!

Have you ever asked yourself questions like these: How did our earth come into existence? How did the moon and sun come into being? Where were you before you were born? How did oceans, trees, animals appear on earth? How do your favourite fruits –bananas, cherries, plums– with all their bright colours and pleasant scents grow in black soil? How does a little tiny bee know how to produce delicious honey? How can it build a honeycomb with such astonishingly regular edges? Who was the first human being? Your mom gave birth to you. Yet the first human being could not have had parents. So, how did he come into existence?" In this book you will find the true answers to these questions.

**144 PAGES WITH 282 PICTURES
IN COLOUR**

Colours, patterns, spots, even lines of each living being existing in nature have a meaning. For some species, colours serve as a communication tool; for others, they are a warning against enemies. Whatever the case, these colours are essential for the well-being of living beings. An attentive eye would immediately recognise that not only the living beings, but also everything in nature are just as they should be. Furthermore, he would realise that everything is given to the service of man: the comforting blue colour of the sky, the colourful view of flowers, the bright green trees and meadows, the moon and stars illuminating the world in pitch darkness together with innumerable beauties surrounding man…

**160 PAGES WITH 215 PICTURES IN
COLOUR**

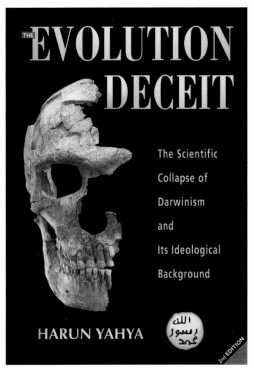

EVOLUTION DECEIT

The Scientific

Collapse of

Darwinism

and

Its Ideological

Background

HARUN YAHYA

Many people think that Darwin's Theory of Evolution is a proven fact. Contrary to this conventional wisdom, recent developments in science completely disprove the theory. The only reason Darwinism is still foisted on people by means of a worldwide propaganda campaign lies in the ideological aspects of the theory. All secular ideologies and philosophies try to provide a basis for themselves by relying on the theory of evolution.

This book clarifies the scientific collapse of the theory of evolution in a way that is detailed but easy to understand. It reveals the frauds and distortions committed by evolutionists to "prove" evolution. Finally it analyzes the powers and motives that strive to keep this theory alive and make people believe in it.

Anyone who wants to learn about the origin of living things, including mankind, needs to read this book.

238 PAGES WITH 166 PICTURES IN COLOUR

One of the purposes why the Qur'an was revealed is to summon people to think about creation and its works. When a person examines his own body or any other living thing in nature, the world or the whole universe, in it he sees a great design, art, plan and intelligence. All this is evidence proving Allah's being, unit, and eternal power.

For Men of Understanding was written to make the reader see and realise some of the evidence of creation in nature. Many living miracles are revealed in the book with hundreds of pictures and brief explanations.

288 PAGES WITH 467 PICTURES IN COLOUR

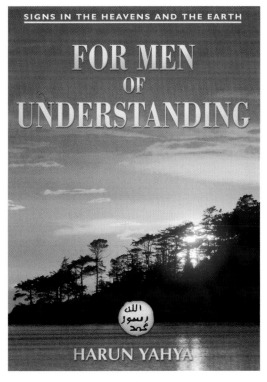

SIGNS IN THE HEAVENS AND THE EARTH

FOR MEN OF UNDERSTANDING

HARUN YAHYA

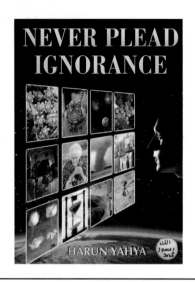

Never plead ignorance of Allah's evident existence, that everything was created by Allah, that everything you own was given to you by Allah for your subsistence, that you will not stay so long in this world, of the reality of death, that the Qur'an is the Book of truth, that you will give account for your deeds, of the voice of your conscience that always invites you to righteousness, of the existence of the hereafter and the day of account, that hell is the eternal home of severe punishment, and of the reality of fate.

112 PAGES WITH 74 PICTURES IN COLOUR

One of the major reasons why people feel a profound sense of attachment to life and cast religion aside is the assumption that life is eternal. Forgetting that death is likely to put an end to this life at any time, man simply believes that he can enjoy a perfect and happy life. Yet he evidently deceives himself. The world is a temporary place specially created by Allah to test man. That is why, it is inherently flawed and far from satisfying man's endless needs and desires. Each and every attraction existing in the world eventually wears out, becomes corrupt, decays and finally disappears. This is the never-changing reality of life.

This book explains this most important essence of life and leads man to ponder the real place to which he belongs, namely the Hereafter.

224 PAGES WITH 144 PICTURES IN COLOUR

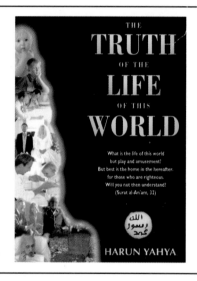

Many societies that rebelled against the will of Allah or regarded His messengers as enemies were wiped off the face of the earth completely... All of them were destroyed—some by a volcanic eruption, some by a disastrous flood, and some by a sand storm...

Perished Nations examines these penalties as revealed in the verses of the Quran and in light of archaeological discoveries.

149 PAGES WITH 73 PICTURES IN COLOUR